"This book is not a collection of techniques or tricks—it uses exercises to help the reader respond to God's direction in a way that is *transformational*. It will help you become more compassionate and sensitive, helping you form deeper relationships."

—Steven L. Brown, MD, PhD, author
of *Navigating the Medical Maze*

"Many of us enter conversations awaiting the moment to jump in with our own story, and completely miss opportunities to listen. This book teaches you how to honor another's story and ask the kind of questions that deepen understanding. *How to Listen So People Will Talk* should be required reading for every doctor, counselor, teacher, and parent."

—Saundra Dalton-Smith, MD, physician, speaker,
author, and founder of I Choose My Best Life

"In a world where everyone is talking, tempers are flaring, emotions are raging, and relationships are spinning out of control, someone has to start listening! Becky Harling knows how to listen so people open up, dialogue, connect, and care for one another. I know because Becky has listened to me—with her HEART! With wisdom and wit, Becky can help all ˄f ˄s learn to listen so we can LOVE the people in our w˄˄ˑ

˄ooks including bestselling
˄omen Are Like Spaghetti

"Do yo˄ ˄ecky Harling unlocks
the secre˄ ˄onal well-being: attentive listening. If ˄ ˄nger marriage, want your parenting to flourish, or ˄ ˄or deeper, more meaningful friendships, ponder the principles of *How to Listen So People Will Talk*."

—Greg and Julie Gorman, authors of *Two Are
Better Than One*, #MarriedForAPurpose

"Becky Harling is a woman of integrity committed to personal growth, so when her daughter confronted her on her listening skills, she knew she needed to change. A passionate speaker, author, and coach, Becky loves helping others reach their God-given potential."

—Dr. Jim Garlow, author and senior pastor
of Skyline Church, La Mesa, California

"I couldn't help but think of a few people who would greatly benefit from reading this book, only to come to a stark realization that I too tend to approach many conversations with my own agenda. Becky challenges all of us to become better listeners by offering some valuable insights and exercises to build the very foundation in developing this important character trait. Get ready to be transformed!"

—Dilip Joseph, author of *Kidnapped by the Taliban*

"If you long for better relationships, read this book. Becky Harling is a master communicator—and in this book she reveals the God-honoring steps we can take to become listeners who help others to share their stories, speak honestly, and feel understood. Each chapter will assist you in identifying a specific skill you can work on that will transform the way you connect with people. Use this book for personal study or bring a group of your friends together and explore how you can develop even stronger interaction with each other as you learn to listen so people will talk."

—Carol Kent, speaker and author of *Speak Up with Confidence*

"We live in a time that affords us endless opportunities to spout our opinions to anyone who will listen. But at what cost to our own soul? And how do these one-way conversations impact our relationships and even our perspective? My friend Becky Harling has written a countercultural book that feels like a word in due season. We can't grow if we're not willing to listen; we can't grow our relationships with others if we're not truly hearing them. Yet there's an art to listening, things we need to guard against when the other person has the floor. If you long to take your spiritual growth to another level, it's time to learn the art of listening. And you've come to the right place."

—Susie Larson, talk-show host, national speaker,
author of *Your Powerful Prayers*

"In a world where everyone is straining to be heard, Becky Harling takes the countercultural approach of showing up and actually listening. If you are longing to know and be known by those you love, *How to Listen So People Will Talk* will not only change your conversations, it will change your relationships. Highly recommended."

—Kathi Lipp, author of *Overwhelmed*

"Becky gets it right again! From her years as a pastor's wife, a mother, and a valued friend, Becky opens up her heart and shares generous wisdom. If you are frustrated with your ability to connect with others, this book will be a source of joy and practical solutions!"

—Carol McLeod, president and founder, Just Joy! Ministries

"*How to Listen So People Will Talk* reminds us that listening is a personal ministry that we must cultivate and nurture. Grounded in God's word, Becky Harling has written a book that is insightful, enlightening, and full of wisdom."

—Ellie Nieves, president and CEO, Leadership Strategies for Women, LLC

"Learning how to speak more powerfully is a common topic for work and personal life, but what about powerful listening? This book will help you shift your focus to this important lost art. As you practice the listening exercises in these pages, the quality of your relationships will skyrocket."

—Arlene Pellicane, speaker and author of *31 Days to Becoming a Happy Wife*

"We all know how to talk, but how few of us know how to listen well. It is impossible to read this book without learning specific skills that will make you a better spouse, friend, parent, and representative of Jesus."

—Dr. Juli Slattery, psychologist and president of Authentic Intimacy

"Becky Harling's book *How to Listen So People Will Talk* is filled with fresh insights and vivid illustrations to empower you to create better understanding and stronger bonds."

—Linda Evans Shepherd, author
of *Winning Your Daily Spiritual Battles*

"We all desire to be heard. In fact, being loved and being heard feel the same. As a spouse, parent, co-worker, sibling, or friend, the greatest gift we can give is our full attention. Becky masterfully weaves stories, hands-on tools, and brilliant devotional moments to teach us how to listen."

—Rick Whitted, author of *Outgrow Your Space at Work:
How To Thrive at Work and Build a Successful Career*

how to
listen
so people will
talk

how to
listen
so people will
talk

Build Stronger Communication
and Deeper Connections

Becky Harling

BETHANYHOUSE
a division of Baker Publishing Group
Minneapolis, Minnesota

Published by Bethany House Publishers
11400 Hampshire Avenue South
Bloomington, Minnesota 55438
www.bethanyhouse.com

Bethany House Publishers is a division of
Baker Publishing Group, Grand Rapids, Michigan

Printed in the United States of America

Library of Congress Control Number: 2017936684

ISBN 978-0-7642-1944-3

Unless otherwise indicated, Scripture quotations are from the Holy Bible, New International Version®. NIV®. Copyright © 1973, 1978, 1984, 2011 by Biblica, Inc.™ Used by permission of Zondervan. All rights reserved worldwide. www.zondervan.com

Scripture quotations labeled ESV are from The Holy Bible, English Standard Version® (ESV®), copyright © 2001 by Crossway, a publishing ministry of Good News Publishers. Used by permission. All rights reserved. ESV Text Edition: 2011

Scripture quotations labeled NLT are from the *Holy Bible*, New Living Translation, copyright © 1996, 2004, 2015 by Tyndale House Foundation. Used by permission of Tyndale House Publishers, Inc., Carol Stream, Illinois 60188. All rights reserved.

Scripture quotations labeled THE MESSAGE are from THE MESSAGE. Copyright © by Eugene H. Peterson 1993, 1994, 1995, 1996, 2000, 2001, 2002. Used by permission of NavPress. All rights reserved. Represented by Tyndale House Publishers, Inc.

Cover design by Greg Jackson, Thinkpen Design, Inc.

Author is represented by The Blythe Daniel Agency.

17 18 19 20 21 22 23   7 6 5 4 3 2 1

This book is dedicated to my
precious daughter,

Bethany Lindgren.

Bethany, I'm so thankful that you found
the courage to honestly challenge me
to become a more attentive listener.

I love you and have the deepest respect
for how you listen to others.

Truly you model what it looks like
to listen to others like Jesus.

I love you!

Contents

1

I Dare You to Ask!

Let the wise listen and add to their learning.
—Proverbs 1:5

I'm convinced that until we risk asking for honest feedback, we can't grow. And even though we want personal growth, it can sure feel painful, right? I was committed to personal growth. I just hadn't anticipated the pain when I asked my teen daughter one crucial question: "Do you think I listen well?"

I expected the conversation to go much differently. Honestly, I was expecting rave reviews, but that's not exactly the way the conversation went. Note to self: Don't ask your kids their opinion unless you're prepared for what they really think! But I *had* asked, and she had answered. "Well . . . (long pause). Sometimes you listen well. But you seem distracted a lot. Often you dive in with your own story or interrupt. Sometimes you give advice and I just want you to listen. I want to feel validated."

Later that night I lay in bed processing my questions internally. *What did she mean? Am I really that self-focused that I dive in with my own stories, taking away from hers?* And then there was the whole question of advice. *Aren't mothers supposed to give advice? I mean, we have so much wisdom. How do I validate if I don't agree with what she's feeling? And am I really that distracted?* She was right. I did sometimes interrupt, but doesn't everybody interrupt at times? I felt pretty sure I was better than most moms. Then it dawned on me. An aha moment: *I'm being defensive! Arrghhh. Help, God!*

That conversation prompted me to come to a startling realization: I have a listening problem. And I'm guessing you might as well. That's probably why you're curious about this book. It could be that someone's told you that you don't listen well. Or you've simply noticed that those closest to you aren't talking as much. They seem to confide in others rather than you.

I don't know about you, but whenever I process a difficult conversation, I pray. It helps me to talk through all my feelings with the Lord. So the moment I realized how defensive I felt, I knew I needed to pray. *Lord, this is hard. But Bethany's right, isn't she? I want to feel like I'm being a great listener, but I also want to receive truth. I long to be self-aware, not self-focused. But honestly, I love to talk! You know, God. You created me to be an extrovert. Could this be your fault? Uh-oh. Defensive again. Lord, I confess to you that I have been self-focused. Forgive me. Search my heart and uproot selfishness. I love Bethany and I want her to feel heard. Show me how to listen.*

That little prayer was the beginning of my journey to becoming a more attentive and loving listener by watching what I say when I'm talking with someone who is confiding in me. And since I'm committed to authenticity, I'll tell you honestly that I'm still growing and it's not always easy. Some days I'm a much better listener than others. Aren't we all?! But I'm improving and growing in this area because my relationships are important to me. I want people in my life to feel heard and loved, don't you? I've seen that the effort I've put into listening is paying off, and I know that's possible for you as well.

Enough About Me, Let's Talk About You!

As I've shared about me, something's probably come up in your mind that reminded you of a conversation you had where you blew it in the listening department. Maybe you realized you didn't really listen to your co-worker or neighbor the other day when they opened up about a problem they're facing. Or maybe you were spacing out while your friend was telling you about a new dream she has. Or maybe when your kids were talking to you, you were scanning Facebook posts. So let's talk about you. How are you doing in the listening realm? How would others rate you as a listener? Would you dare to ask those closest to you how well they think you listen? It's scary, I know, to invite that kind of feedback. But can you imagine how much you might grow if you were willing to take that risk? How would your spouse, friend, boss, or co-worker react if you asked that question? Powerful stuff!

Maybe you're like a lady I met a few years ago who said to me, "I can't help it. I'm only good to listen for about fifteen seconds." Really? That's just an excuse for not wanting to put in the effort. Reflect for a moment or two and ask yourself honestly:

- Do my loved ones feel safe enough to express their hearts, or are they afraid I'll dive in with unwanted and unsolicited advice?
- When I'm with a friend at lunch, do I text or check social media while she's talking?
- How would my co-workers rate me as a listener?

I'm not trying to lay a guilt trip on you. I'm just trying to encourage you to examine your listenership and be willing to grow. Because here's the deal: People feel more loved and valued if we are actively and attentively listening to them. So why don't we take listening more seriously?

We may know that listening is important, but without even being aware, we interrupt, dive in with our own stories, give unwanted

15

advice, or simply space out. It makes sense because we've got stimulation bombarding us all day long. We're more distracted than ever. It's become our normal. As a result, we're losing our ability to be fully present and attentive to others because we've bought in to the myth of multitasking. It's hard to listen when you know you have one minute to send an email before you leave, or dinner needs to be ready in five. I know, because I'm guilty too.

When I was raising my kids, I prided myself on the fact that I could cook dinner, help with homework, and talk on the phone all at the same time. Now I realize that's not something to be proud of. Looking back, I did a disservice to my kids and to whomever I was talking with on the phone. And dinner—well, let's just say I had a few burned failures.

My theory is that often we're not aware of our own shortcomings and weaknesses. But our relationships are important to us. That's why I want to dare you to ask honestly: "Do you think I listen well?"

You'll Need a Plan

When I realized I needed a growth plan for listening, I turned to the Bible. I learned that there are at least seventy verses in the Bible that use the word *listen* or talk about listening in some form. Wow! Apparently God wants us to hear Him on this topic! Many of those verses are found in the book of Proverbs, which was written by Solomon, who was considered the wisest man of his time. Did you know that this tiny Old Testament book is loaded with relational wisdom? Here are just a few examples:

- "Let the wise listen and add to their learning" (Proverbs 1:5).
- "Turning your ear to wisdom and applying your heart to understanding" (Proverbs 2:2).
- "To answer before listening—that is folly and shame" (Proverbs 18:13).

- "The wise woman builds her house, but with her own hands the foolish one tears hers down" (Proverbs 14:1).

I wanted to be a wise woman who listened and invested in her relationships. Proverbs seemed to offer just the plan I needed. As I read and re-read this short book, I began to pull out practical principles that I could immediately put into practice. They became my plan for personal growth in the realm of listening. And you know what? As I faithfully practiced my plan, my relationships gradually began to improve.

Friend, just like I needed a plan, *you* need a plan. You won't become an effective listener without intentionality because listening doesn't come naturally. As humans, we're self-focused. But it's possible to change! It'll take practice and patience, but it's worth the effort, because how you listen not only deepens your relationships, it's also important to God.

God created us for relationship. We weren't meant to live our lives alone. We were designed to mirror the image of a relational God, One who communicates and connects with others. This is why we naturally crave love and attention from others, and they naturally crave love and attention from us. Just as God listens to us, we are designed to imitate Him and listen to others. Not only does this meet the need for love and attention in the person talking, but it meets our need to feel loved and connected as well.

American poet and writer Maya Angelou said, "The most called-upon prerequisite of a friend is an accessible ear."[1] Do you want to cultivate deep friendships? Then learn to listen. I guarantee you'll feel happier, more connected, and more valuable. The bottom line is that people are drawn to those who will listen to them. Learning to listen will deepen your relationships, establish your credibility, and give you a reputation of being wise. Wow! What a win.

Jesus modeled what we read about relational wisdom in Proverbs. Let's look at a passage where Jesus specifically addresses listening.

Consider Carefully How You Listen

At one point Jesus wasn't sure those following Him were understanding His message, so He gave them a stern warning about their ability to listen.

Turning to His followers, Jesus instructed, "Therefore consider carefully how you listen" (Luke 8:18). We need to consider our listening skills. He calls us to look at ourselves and give some thought to how we listen to others. As His followers, we are called to love others radically. "As I have loved you, so you must love one another" (John 13:34). Loving includes listening.

As I think about the different relationships I enjoy, whether my husband, my kids, my grandkids, my friends, my co-workers, or my neighbors, I want each person to feel valued and loved. Isn't that the way you want others to feel? If each person in your life felt valued and loved, they would naturally open up more to you, and everyone would benefit from a deeper relationship.

Pause and think for a moment. Do you provide a safe listening ear for people? It's a high calling, isn't it? As those who follow Christ, we aren't often known for creating a safe place for broken people to express and process their thoughts and ideas. Do we provide a safe place for our family, co-workers, and friends to share their fears? Or are people reluctant to share their thoughts for fear they'll be judged? I agree with Dietrich Bonhoeffer, who reminded us, "Christians have forgotten that the ministry of listening has been committed to them by Him who is Himself the great listener and whose work they should share. We should listen with the ears of God that we may speak the Word of God."[2] Friend, how can we effectively minister to and encourage others if we aren't listening? The need is urgent. So what do ya say? Let's figure this out!

Our family, friends, neighbors, and even strangers all need to feel valued and heard. Honestly, I haven't always done this well, but I've been asking the Lord to change me because I am convinced people feel lonely when no one listens to them.

I had a neighbor whom I mistakenly thought didn't like me. I waved and called out to her often, receiving no response in return. I mistakenly thought for a while, *Maybe she doesn't speak English.* One evening I went out to take a walk and she was coming out of her house. I waved and she said she wanted to walk with me. I was a bit shocked! But I agreed and off we went. While we walked for several miles, this precious woman poured out her heart. Her husband had been in the military, and they had married while he was serving overseas. She married young and they were very much in love. He took care of her and provided for her in every way. Her husband had died a few years earlier, and she told me how lonely it had been for her. She has never fully adjusted to his death. Her two grown children both serve in the military and don't live nearby. When I left her that night, she told me how much she enjoyed our time together.

The next day I called out to her, as I had done so many times before. When she didn't answer, I looked a little closer and realized she had earphones on and was listening to music! It dawned on me in that moment that the times I had called out to her, she had never even heard me. I asked the Lord that day to teach me not to make assumptions about people, but rather to take initiative with people to simply listen.

I once saw a homeless man with a sign that read, "Will listen for $5 per half hour." What a brilliant business plan! That guy is probably a millionaire by now. The homeless man had tapped in to a felt need. Most people are too rushed or distracted to take time to listen. How sad that people need to pay to feel like someone is listening.

As those who claim to love and follow Jesus, we're the ones who should be leading the way and listening to people. Right? If not us, then who? Wouldn't it be great if Christians had the reputation of being great listeners? What does it take for us to change?

Growth involves intentionality. Keep a listening journal as you progress through this book. You might consider some of the following questions:

1. How did I hear God's voice this week?
2. What patterns did I observe in my own heart that might get in the way of being an effective listener?
3. What question did I ask that helped me to understand someone better?
4. What do I need to do differently next time to help me understand more?
5. What action do I need to take to follow up on a conversation from this week?

I'm guessing that, like me, you value your relationships. As you honestly examine your abilities as a listener and cooperate with the Holy Spirit, He will reshape your listening skills, and your relationships will improve. But you have to be willing.

Think about a relationship that's very important to you that you'd like to see improve. It could be with your husband, a parent, your child, or a close friend. Consider for a moment how much you value that connection. In your journal, write down why that relationship is so important to you. Keep that person in mind as you move through the rest of this book. Whenever you feel like the principles in the book are too challenging, or you feel discouraged and ready to give up with that person, ask the Lord to remind you of how important that bond is to you and how much listening will add value to his or her life and your own. The bottom line is this, friend: If you value your relationships, you'll be willing to work at listening so that others around you will feel heard.

Are You Ready to Get Started?

As we move through the rest of this book, we're going to study biblically based, practical listening skills. If you embrace these skills, your relationships will improve! Don't worry, the principles we'll look at aren't complicated. But they do take practice. I promise you, if you faithfully practice and press into the Holy Spirit as your guide in listening, you will see almost an immediate difference in your interactions with others.

We're going to look at how to:

- Raise your self-awareness
- Honor another's story
- Silence your inner "fixer"
- Ask great questions
- Offer empathy and validate feelings
- Monitor your nonverbal signals
- Seek to understand in a conflict
- Let go of distractions
- Be available

At the end of each chapter you'll find a section called "Exercises to Strengthen Your Ear." Included in this section will be questions and activities divided into three categories: Listening to God, Listening to Your Heart, and Listening to Others.

Listening is like a muscle. The more we develop and train, the stronger our listening skills will become and the more effective we'll become as listeners. I encourage you to open your journal as you move through these exercises so that you can write down your observations about your progress and see how you are doing along the way. I will encourage you to share some of your journal entries with someone you are intentionally trying to be a better listener to in this season of your life.

So here's our first set of exercises. Jesus not only wants to transform your listening skills, but also to use you to make an impact on the lives you intersect with on a daily basis. You have all that you need to do this—ears and an open heart. Let's get started!

Strengthen Your Ear

Listening to God

1. Listening *to* God is foundational to being able to listen *like* God. One of the ways we can prepare our hearts to listen to God is through worship. Listen to "Holy Spirit" by Kari Jobe and Cody Carnes. As you listen, ask the Holy Spirit to fill your mind with only thoughts that are from Him. After you listen to the song, read John 6:45. Then answer in a journal the following questions:
   - What are some tangible ways to listen to God's voice?
   - In what ways have you heard God's voice in the past?

2. Read 1 Samuel 3:1–14. How did Samuel hear God's voice? What lesson is there for you in this passage?

3. Sit quietly with your eyes closed for at least three minutes. Ask the Lord to speak to you. He might lay something on your heart or bring to your mind a thought from the Scripture you just read. Write down what you felt He spoke.

Listening to Your Heart

Listening to your heart is focused on teaching you to understand what's in your heart. Until people really understand what's in their own hearts, they're often unable to focus their attention on others because, to put it bluntly, their own emotional baggage keeps coming up in their conversations.

Take a few minutes to sit still and ask yourself these questions:

- *Am I worried about anything?* Make a list of all your worries and then release them one by one to the Lord.
- *Am I feeling stressed or overwhelmed?* What are the things that are making you feel stressed or overwhelmed? Make a list.
- *What are some of the destructive patterns that often surface when I am trying to listen to someone?* For example: Do you interrupt? Give unsolicited advice? Try to fix other people's emotions?
- Write out a prayer asking the Lord to help you to stop whatever pattern is surfacing most often. Ask the Lord to remind you throughout the day to be intentional while you're listening to others, to change that destructive pattern.

Listening to Others

In this section I'll give exercises to help you try out your new skills with others. Here are a few to get you started:

- Ask someone close to you what he or she enjoys most about his or her job. As you listen, practice staying focused and fully attentive. Don't interrupt or dive in with a story of your own. Simply listen.
- When your spouse comes home from work or when you get together with a close friend this week, ask him or her to tell you the highlights of their day. While he or she are talking, invite them to tell you more. Verbalize how deeply you appreciate them taking the time to share their thoughts and feelings.

I Dare You

As we close this chapter, I want to challenge you to ask three people who are close to you to take the following survey to rate how you are as a listener. Explain to them that you are working on your listening skills because you value your relationship with them. Clarify that you need their help because you're not always sure how you come across to others in the realm of listening. Then ask them to fill out the simple survey.

I know it might feel scary, but we can't grow if we don't face the truth. Only give the survey to people you really want to invest in, and ask them to please be honest with you. If they rate you low on some part of your listening ability, don't argue or push back on their thoughts. Simply say, "Thank you for being honest with me." Save the survey and, after progressing through this book, give them the survey again and ask them if they've seen any growth on your part.

As you look at the initial feedback from the survey, you might pray this prayer:

Lord, as I reflect on my listening survey results, I realize I have some growing to do. Holy Spirit, over the next few weeks, as I study listening skills from your perspective, I pray that you would change my heart. Shift my focus from myself to others. Fill me with your heart for others. Teach me how to listen and love those closest to me, as well as neighbors and acquaintances. I surrender my ears for a total renovation. Lord, my heart's desire is to learn to listen like Jesus.

After you give this survey, create the space to reflect on the results to see where you may need to pour some extra time into developing yourself as a listener. Often there is a pattern that we can see through someone else's eyes that's so crucial for our growth. Choose to see the positives in this exercise. Look at what you can learn about yourself from someone else's perspective, rather than think, *Oh no, the truth is coming out about me.* Think of it as an opportunity to invest in an area of your life that sets you apart from others—a magnetic attraction you will possess because you have learned to listen well. Have fun, and anticipate good things coming from this!

Survey—How Would You Rank Me as a Listener?

I am seeking to improve my listening skills because I deeply value my relationship with you. Would you take a few moments to answer these questions? Circle the answer that best fits. Please give me honest feedback.

	Rarely	Sometimes	Often
1. I am guilty of interrupting.	☐	☐	☐
2. I am present when you talk—not texting, checking email, or looking at social media.	☐	☐	☐
3. I dive in with my own story or experience.	☐	☐	☐
4. I give unsolicited advice.	☐	☐	☐
5. I validate your feelings.	☐	☐	☐
6. My body language invites you to tell me more.	☐	☐	☐
7. I seem defensive when my opinions are challenged.	☐	☐	☐
8. When you communicate with me you feel hurried.	☐	☐	☐
9. When we disagree I offer understanding.	☐	☐	☐
10. You feel safe to share your feelings with me.	☐	☐	☐

2

Raise Your Self-Awareness

Humility brings grace to our need, and grace alone
can change our hearts. Humility, therefore, is the sub-
structure of transformation.

—Francis Frangipane

Seated in a quiet coffee shop, a friend and I were sharing our
hearts. As rich and flavorful as the dark espresso we were sipping, our conversation felt full and refreshing. We chatted about
our walks with God, our families, our hardships, ministries, and
dreams until we were abruptly interrupted. Right as my friend
was sharing extremely vulnerable thoughts about her journey with
breast cancer, a former acquaintance of mine walked up to our
table and began talking. Like a flood of water from a fire hydrant,
words gushed out about upcoming events and stress—lots of stress!
When my acquaintance finally walked away, I felt frustrated, em-
barrassed, and a bit unsure of how to re-engage my friend in our
original conversation.

Later, I spent some time reflecting. I'm pretty sure that my acquaintance had no idea how she came across. Her heart is good and she

did have a lot of stress going on. Unfortunately, she was completely unaware. I wondered what she was hoping for out of that conversation. Validation? Affirmation? But the more I thought about it, the more I realized that to my horror, *I've done the very same thing.*

Completely un-self-aware, I walked into church, stressed out because of impending deadlines. The moment I saw one of my friends, I dove into what was due when and what I had coming up. Quietly and graciously my friend excused herself to go get her kids. It wasn't until much later that I cringed internally when I realized how I had come across. As I thought back, I asked myself, "What was I hoping for out of the conversation?"

You've probably done something similar. It's so easy to talk all about how busy and stressed out we are rather than listening to others. Our primary focus seems to be ourselves, and that inevitably comes out of our mouths. The bottom line is we all crave attention and affirmation. It's my theory that we all have a little narcissist tucked way down deep inside who's dying to feel heard and affirmed! Truthfully, we don't often recognize how we're coming across.

What Does It Mean to Be Self-Aware?

How do we become self-aware enough to understand our own shortcomings in the listening category, but not become self-focused and sabotage our efforts to become better listeners? Self-awareness is not something I hear discussed in the Christian world very often. But I believe it's important because Jesus was very self-aware. He knew who He was and why He had come. So what does it mean to be self-aware?

Let's keep things simple. To be self-aware means you are aware of what's going on in your heart, how you're coming across to others, and where you might need to change. You have a humble view of yourself, and you recognize you're not perfect.

Why is it important to be self-aware? Because in a nutshell, God's primary agenda in your life is to change you so that you

27

become more like Jesus (Romans 8:29). How can you cooperate with Him if you're not aware of your weaknesses and strengths?

I believe it's a heart issue. Solomon instructed, "From a wise mind comes wise speech" (Proverbs 16:23 NLT). Jesus echoed the writer of Proverbs and said, "For out of the abundance of the heart the mouth speaks" (Matthew 12:34 ESV). If you don't know what's going on in your heart, you're liable to mess up with your mouth! I would also like to suggest that if you don't know what's going on in your heart, you won't be able to listen well. It's my conviction that in order to grow in our ability to listen to others, we've got to become more self-aware, and that takes a humble heart.

Tricky Business

Understanding what's in your heart can be a bit tricky, can't it? Our hearts hold love and hatred, fear and courage, altruism and egotism. Proverbs 4:23 teaches us that from the heart flows the "spring of life" (ESV) while Jeremiah teaches us that "the heart is deceitful" (17:9). It's easy to go through the whole day and be unaware of the issues you've got going on in your heart until *bam!* Those issues come out of your mouth and you realize you're not listening. I have realized this in my own life all too often.

I start my day with the best of intentions. But then a conversation happens and I find myself wanting to be viewed as the expert or acting as the fact police. Later I wonder, *Where did those feelings come from?* Or I'll get into an argument with my husband and the walls of defensiveness form a soundproof space around my mind that prevents me from really hearing and understanding. With further reflection I wonder, *Why did I build that wall?*

Can you relate? Maybe your teen comes home from school and begins the conversation with these words: "Don't say no right away like you always do. . . ." Immediately, your defenses go up and your listening ear tunes out. Before your teen even finishes the first sentence, you've decided *no* is the right answer. Later you regret your decision, realizing that you might be sacrificing the relationship with your teen because of your desire to have control.

You walk in on a conversation at work where two of your co-workers are talking politics. Throwing caution to the wind, you dive in with your opinions, your insights, and your preferences, though no one has asked you. You're dying to be viewed as a leader, but no one seems willing to follow. Could it be that they perceive you as someone not willing to listen? Are you aware of how you come across?

Honestly, it's impossible to be a good listener without developing a humble spirit. Think about it. When you're listening and fully engaged, you allow the other person to have all the attention. Listening forces you to lay aside your agenda. It challenges you to let go of your need to share your opinions, theories, and assumptions in favor of listening to another's feelings, thoughts, and sentiments. That decision can only come from a heart of humility.

Understanding Humility

Humility starts with self-awareness. Understanding both your strengths and your weaknesses, you're able to commit to personal growth. The idea of growing in our strengths feels exciting, but personal growth in the area of our weaknesses? Not so much! Change often means pain. If we're going to become the listeners God wants us to be, we've got to be able to admit our weaknesses. Only as we are brave enough to face the truth about our weaknesses can we cooperate with God in the transformation process He envisions for our lives.

If I were to define humility, here's how I would define it:

Humility is understanding who you are in Christ, letting go of the need to flaunt your gifts or promote yourself at the expense of others.

God wants to see Christ-like humility developed in our lives. He wants us to become more like His Son Jesus, whose whole life spoke a message of humility. The apostle Paul wrote that to be like Jesus, we're to clothe ourselves with humility (Colossians 3:12).

Putting on humility might seem a bit weird to us. We dress to project an image that speaks significance. I mean, who doesn't appreciate a killer outfit that builds your confidence? I sure do! Paul's not bashing our clothing choices. He's suggesting that just as we invest in our clothes, we also purposefully invest in cultivating an attitude of humility. Since our hearts are so complicated, what does it look like to develop humility? Let's go back to Jesus.

Jesus was important in every sense of the word. He had every reason to be the expert and never listen to anyone. But instead He chose to humble himself and become a servant (Philippians 2:5–8). He was completely self-aware but not self-focused. He's the One who said, "I and the Father are one" (John 10:30). His humility was wrapped up in His relationship with the Father. He knew beyond a shadow of a doubt that He was deeply loved. When you know you're deeply loved it's a whole lot easier to be humble.

When I know God the Father completely and wholly loves me, I have dignity and worth as His beloved child.

- Because I am God's beloved child, I don't need to prove myself. I have worth. I don't need to be seen as the expert.
- Because God sees everything I'm going through and understands, I don't need continual validation.
- Because God is attentive to my every breath, I don't need to be the center of attention.
- Because God fills me with courage, I don't need to operate out of fear in conversation.
- Because God is in control, I don't need to engage in power struggles.

Operating out of that secure core, I am able to let go of the need to be important, and defer to the opinions of others. I don't have to prove them wrong or assert that my opinion is the only right one. Instead, I allow others to be the center of attention without competing for the limelight. I ask God to fill me with a sense of His love, so that out of the overflow of a full heart I let someone else be the star because I value my relationship with that person.

My friend Harry is a great example of this. Though Harry had always been successful in ministry, he subconsciously felt he had to earn God's love. Probably Harry wasn't even aware he felt that way. But after a lengthy battle with depression, Harry pursued a deeper revelation of Christ's love. He and his wife, Patty, buried themselves in the Gospels, asking that the Holy Spirit would reveal to them the depth of God's love. As their hearts plumbed the depths of Christ's love, Harry began to change. He became less obsessed with proving himself as a strong leader. Instead, he began to simply serve others and listen to them. This included moving with Patty to India to serve the Dalit people.

Recently, Harry went home to be with the Lord. At his memorial service his brother commented that after Harry had a deeper revelation of Christ's love, he was "less driven and more able to simply listen to others." What changed Harry? A fresh revelation of Christ's love clothed Harry in humility and transformed him into a leader who listened.

Jesus dressed himself in humility because He prioritized His relationship with His Father and with us. His desire is that His dynamic and consuming love transforms us so that we can prioritize our relationships with others by adopting His attitude. But that will take intentionality on our part. In order to humbly listen to others, we need to increase our self-awareness and then surrender our right to be the expert.

The best way I know to become more self-aware is to learn the art of reflective listening. In other words, listen to your heart and figure out what's going on inside. Only then will you be able to change old patterns of behavior.

Listen to Your Heart

Please understand that when I say listen to your heart, I'm not saying do whatever your heart tells you to do. No. I'm saying develop the practice of reflective listening so that you understand more clearly what's driving your internal choices. As author and consultant John Savage writes, "If you keep in touch with what is going on inside yourself while you are listening, there is a better chance of guessing what is going on in the other. So be aware of your own inner condition."[1] Develop the regular practice of doing an internal check by reflecting on what's in your heart. Reflective listening will help you find lurking motives such as jealousy, insecurity, and the quest for validation or power. Any one of those could easily sabotage your listening efforts, so it's important that you become self-aware.

Here are a few questions designed to guide your reflective listening to discover the motives driving you. My suggestion is that you create the space to reflect on each of these questions. Please don't rush. Take your time.

When I said _____, what response was I looking for?

Think through some recent conversations you've had with family, friends, neighbors, or co-workers. For example, Brielle is a mom of three young toddlers. In the thick of parenting young children, Brielle often feels she doesn't accomplish much. The other day when her husband, Derek, got home from work and asked how her day was, Brielle rattled off a long list of activities. Derek really wasn't looking for that much detail. As Brielle reflected back on the conversation and asked herself, "What response was I looking for?" she realized she was hoping Derek would applaud her efforts and validate how challenging her day had been.

When I ask myself, "What response was I looking for?" it's helpful for me to first ask, "What was I feeling?" If I can name what I was feeling at the time, then it's usually a whole lot easier for me to identify what I was looking for from the other person. For example, when I dumped all my feelings on my friend at church,

I realized with a little reflection that I was feeling overwhelmed. As I reflected on that feeling, I was then able to identify that I was looking for validation and the encouragement that I could do what was being required of me.

This two-step process, "What was I feeling? What was I looking for?" helps me in many situations. Here's an illustration: My husband, Steve, and I were out to dinner, and Steve was doing a lot of verbal processing about a new job offer. I was trying to listen empathetically but kept finding myself getting annoyed. Steve was trying to figure out why I was getting annoyed, because the job change would be huge for us. With further reflection I was able to identify my feeling: insecurity. Silly, I know, but hang with me. I had been having a bad body image day and so I had put a lot of effort into my makeup and hair, etc. Steve, caught up in his job opportunity, hadn't even noticed. Later, as I reflected on what I felt and what I had been hoping for, I realized I had been hoping Steve would say something like, "Wow, babe, you look awesome tonight. I think you're beautiful!" As I realized that was what I was hoping for, I was able to offer Steve grace and understanding, knowing he felt stressed and was hoping for validation himself, and needed someone to process his feelings with.

Why did I respond that way?

Make a list of the people closest to you. Your list might include parents, spouse, siblings, children, grandchildren, friends, or others. As you consider each person on your list, reflect back on your most recent conversations with them. Did you offer unsolicited advice? Why? What motivated you to do that? Please note: If you are still actively parenting, you will need to give instruction and advice to your kids. Therefore, instead of evaluating *if* you gave advice, evaluate the *method* you used to give instruction. Ask, *Did the method I use feel like an attack to my child? Is there something different I might try?* For example, when we were raising teens, I learned that I had to monitor my facial expressions. If my face conveyed shock, my teen shut down. (We'll talk more about that in chapter 9.) Trust me when I say that was a long journey for me!

Here are a few other questions you might consider: Were you fully present when those closest to you were talking, or were you thinking through your to-do list? If you weren't fully present, why not? Were you continually checking email or social media? Why? Was it a desire to be in the know, or to stay connected so you don't feel lonely? Why is that so important to you? You might not even be aware that you're texting while others are talking.

If you are courageous enough, I recommend that you ask each one on your list if they feel heard by you. If they don't, what can you do differently?

What fears have caused me to grow defensive in the past?

Whenever you grow defensive in a conversation, it's driven by fear. It could be the fear of losing control, fear of failure, fear of embarrassment, fear of not having a voice, or fear of not being respected. Whatever the fear, some part of you feels threatened, and as a result you put up walls to guard your heart. But the instant you become defensive, you're unable to listen effectively. Instead, you're defending your heart. Let me give you an example.

Within the realm of marriage, money is often a difficult topic. This was the case for Barb and Tom. Early in their marriage, Tom was very controlling of the finances and Barb felt she had no voice. Fights erupted often since the two could not agree on how and when to spend. About ten years into their marriage, Tom and Barb decided to get some counseling. The counselor helped them agree on a spending budget, which gave voice to Barb and greatly alleviated the arguments. However, every now and then, Barb still found herself becoming defensive during discussions involving money. As she began to become more self-aware, she realized that her defensiveness was linked to the fear that she would not have a voice in financial decision making. Once Barb realized her trigger, she began to pause in financial discussions, pray, and then remind herself that she and Tom were on the same team. Tom was no longer trying to trump her with his opinions. When Barb let go of defensiveness, she was able to focus on solving whatever financial issue was at hand.

Similarly, if you're a parent and one child continually negotiates with you, it's easy to go on the defensive the moment you feel a conversation is headed toward an argument. Driven by the fear that your child is out of control, you might come down too hard, trying to regain control. Instead, may I suggest you pause, ask God to quiet your fears, and then calmly respond to your child.

Maybe at work you find yourself in a team meeting and you begin to feel fearful that your opinion will not be heard. That fear creates defensiveness, so what do you do? You start talking. Fast. Frantic. Frenzied. You want to be sure your voice is heard. But in all your talking, you've stopped listening, and as a result you've given up your voice because everyone around the table has tuned you out. Generally speaking, the person who talks the most in a meeting is often the person with the greatest insecurities. Do yourself a favor. Ask the Holy Spirit to reveal your fears, and then speak only after you've listened to others. If you want credibility in the workplace, don't talk a lot. Instead, listen and only speak when you have something wise to say.

What signals of stress and exhaustion do I need to recognize in myself in order to set better boundaries?

I don't know anyone who listens effectively when they feel stressed out or exhausted. When you feel stressed out, what's your M.O.? Do you snap at others? Talk faster? Tune out? Shut down? Or perhaps all of those!

Honestly, I know that I don't listen well when I feel stressed. I tend to talk faster and tune out what's going on around me. That means when the deadlines are piling up and I feel there aren't enough hours in the day, I need to pause. Pray. Stop. Breathe. And ask the Holy Spirit to help me re-tune in to whatever is happening around me. I also know that exhaustion follows close on the heels of stress. In order to avoid complete exhaustion, I need to set boundaries around my schedule so that I allow time for rest and renewal. If I don't, whoever is talking to me gets ripped off because I'm only half there.

Admitting we need rest is both humbling and holy. It forces us to admit that we cannot be the "Savior" to others. Only Jesus can do that. God has designed our bodies to need rest. When we prioritize rest and renewal, we are living in obedience to God's plan, and we create the space in our hearts to be able to listen to others. Even when Jesus lived on earth He was bound by the limitations of a human body, and as such needed rest and renewal. If He needed to set boundaries, how much more do we?

As you become more self-aware, you'll feel a deeper desire for the attitude of Christ to be reflected in your listening. You'll become more willing to lay aside your stuff—whatever's going on in your life—to listen attentively like Christ.

Lay Aside Your Stuff

The apostle Paul had some wise words for those trying to listen. He wrote, "In humility value others above yourselves, not looking to your own interests but each of you to the interests of others. In your relationships with one another, have the same mindset as Christ Jesus" (Philippians 2:3–5). Jesus dressed himself in humility because He prioritized His relationship with us. He invites us to prioritize our relationships by following His example, laying aside our stuff and focusing on the needs of others.

Jesus had more reason to feel stressed out than anyone I know. The religious leaders were always mad at Him and trying to kill Him. He carried the weight of everyone's problems on His shoulders. The crowds continually wanted another miracle. And He knew He would ultimately face death on a cross. Talk about pressure!

Jesus' opinions were right about everything because He was God. He is the only One with the absolute correct view of everything. But even Jesus didn't push His opinions on others. Instead,

He listened and only spoke truth in response. Some of us have strong opinions on everything from raising kids to political parties to how we make coffee. Having a strong opinion on certain things is fine. But that doesn't mean everyone has to agree with you. Humbly lay aside your opinions in favor of listening attentively.

Mother Teresa has always intrigued me because of her godly servant leadership. I recently came across this captivating statement:

> She was a powerful woman who didn't use armies, money or pressure to influence change. Instead, Mother Teresa listened with humility. She set aside her opinions, cast out stereotypes, focused on the moment and acknowledged the troubles of others. She made listening with humility a fine art.[2]

The phrase *listening with humility* strikes me because I realize that was the key to Mother Teresa's influence. She was self-aware. She understood her strengths and weaknesses. Like Jesus, Mother Teresa didn't give up her leadership when she chose humility. Quite the opposite, she strengthened her ability to influence by her choice to listen.

That's what I want in my life, don't you? I want to be able to master the art of listening, but that comes at a cost. It was a cost Mother Teresa was willing to pay. She was willing to put aside her opinions and preferences to embrace a heart of humility.

As we conclude this chapter, I realize once again how important it is to pray the prayer of the psalmist David, "Search me, O God, and know my heart; test me and know my anxious thoughts. Point out anything in me that offends you, and lead me along the path of everlasting life" (Psalm 139:23–24 NLT).

Lord, I want to listen to others with a heart of humility, laying aside my agenda and advice. I realize once again how much further I have to go. Examine my heart. Teach me to become more self-aware, and show me the ways of communication I use that are offensive to others.

Listening to God

1. Read Psalm 139:23–24. In these verses, David writes out a prayer to God expressing his desire for God to help him examine his heart. Write out these verses in your own words, expressing your desire for God to search your heart and show you patterns of listening that He wants to change. (For example, patterns of interrupting, diving in with your own story, etc.) Then sit quietly for three to five minutes. If God brings any patterns to mind, write them down. Assume that God is speaking to you and ask Him to help you change.

2. Read Ephesians 3:17–19. After reading these verses, what do you think God wants you to know about His love for you? How might a deeper understanding of His love help you lay aside your own desire for attention in order to focus completely on another?

Listening to Your Heart

Get alone and take a few unhurried minutes to reflect on the following questions:

3. "When I feel stressed, I _____."
   (Describe your general M.O. when you feel stressed, e.g., you

might write "I talk faster," "I get a sick stomach," or "I rush through life like a crazy person.")

4. How do you think stress affects your ability to listen attentively to others?

5. When you're in a room with people you've never met before, how do you most generally respond?

   A. Meet as many people as possible

   B. Meet one person and ask several questions

   C. Grab a drink and wait for someone to approach with a question

6. Think back over a conversation you have had that left you feeling frustrated. What were you hoping for out of that conversation?

7. What situations are most likely to bring out your desire to be seen as the expert?

8. What situations are most likely to bring out a judgmental attitude in you?

9. How do you want to be remembered at your funeral? What changes might you need to make now to be remembered the way you want to be then?

Listening to Others

10. Intentionally, take a friend to coffee and ask about the stress she is experiencing in her family, her place of work, or her church. As she processes her stress, allow her to dump on you. But do not relate or talk about your stress at any point

in the conversation. Simply keep your focus on your friend and allow her to exhale all her stress.

11. Ask a person close to you—your spouse, your child, a close friend, or a co-worker—their view on a current issue that you feel passionate about. As they share their view, practice listening. Don't give your opinion, even if you disagree. Only listen and practice seeking to understand their view.

3

Honor Another's Story

Thoughts disentangle themselves when they pass over
the lips or through the fingertips.

—Dawson Trotman

As part of my husband, Steve's, sabbatical, we returned to his childhood home in Nigeria. After a very long flight, we landed in Lagos and were graciously met by Amos, our driver. Instantly transported into another world, I tried to take in all the sights, sounds, and smells as we travelled to key places of Steve's childhood.

On our first stop, chickens squawked and African beetles sang as we walked up the path to a tiny house. The owner of the home came out to meet us with a baby on her back and toddlers running barefoot behind. Graciously, she invited us into her humble home. Memories spilled in tears as Steve processed, "This was the room where I slept with my brothers. This was the outdoor fireplace where my little brother's shoes caught on fire. This was where I learned to ride a bike."

I was beginning to understand more of my husband's story, but the most crucial piece of understanding unfolded the following day when we arrived at the boarding school where Steve had been dropped off at age seven. We drove onto the grounds and I watched a transformation in my husband that I had never seen. He was unable to speak; sobs crippled him as he remembered being dropped off all those years ago. Tears flooded his face as he took in the sights: the place by the swing where his parents said good-bye, the dorms with little bunk beds, the confusion over being left mixed with the pressure of "sucking it up," knowing that his parents were doing God's work.

Later, as we sat by ourselves swatting mosquitos and sipping coffee, Steve began to talk. His thoughts and feelings spilled out unhindered, and I knew I was on holy ground. I haven't always listened attentively to my husband, but on that day, I leaned toward Steve and listened with every fiber of my being. I didn't want to miss even one word as he shared his heart.

As Steve talked, I became acquainted with the little blond boy who grew up turning over rocks to look for snakes, swimming in rivers, and chasing monkeys. Vestiges of that little boy now lived in the strong, fearless leader who was my husband. As Steve continued processing his story, I was given a front-row seat to how faith was forged the day he prayed in childlike faith, "God, please. I need to see my parents." Minutes later, his parents and grandparents (who were also missionaries in Nigeria) showed up for an unexpected visit.

I asked him, "How did that impact your faith?"

Steve told me it was the first tangible prayer he remembered God answering.

As he continued processing his time at boarding school, I began to understand more deeply Steve's ambivalent feelings about his childhood: crazy stories about boarding school fun mixed with creepy memories of bullies and severe discipline, deep commitment to the gospel mixed with the profound cost it held for him personally.

Minutes flew by and hours passed. Steve processed and I listened. That afternoon our hearts became more deeply knit as one.

Later that night, it took me a long time to fall asleep. My mind was filled with stories from Steve's childhood. I realized what a privilege it was to be married to my man. The legacy of his grandparents passed down to his parents and then passed down to Steve was remarkable. The commitment to the gospel intermingled with the cost to family life had shaped my husband's heart, our marriage, and how we raised our kids. I finally fell asleep praying, *Lord Jesus, thank you for allowing me the privilege of listening to my husband's story. Thank you for giving me deeper understanding into Steve's childhood. Thank you for connecting our hearts more completely today.*

Why Are Stories Important?

Whether it's the story of your parents, spouse, kids, friends, co-workers, or neighbors, stories bond us in a way that builds deeper community. They help us organize our world and process our feelings and values. They connect us to others and help us communicate how we want to be treated. They give voice to our feelings and words to our desires. Think about it—storytelling starts in childhood. Often that's how we figure out what kids are thinking and feeling.

Recently, my little pre-school-age grandson, Tyler, was using two of his stuffed animals to tell my daughter a story. Ty said, "Mom, Rolly and Polly are happy. They went to Mimi's house for Sunday dinner and then Mimi said they could spend the night!"

After hearing Ty's story, I knew he wanted to have a sleepover at my house.

Storytelling isn't just for kids. It's important for adults too. "Experts consider sharing the story of loss and finding someone to attentively and empathetically listen to be integral in the recovery process."[1] Even in the realm of medical care, storytelling

43

is important. Doctors are now being encouraged to take the time to listen to patients more attentively, listening not only for what's being said but also for what's not being said so that they can provide the best possible medical care. No kidding! Who doesn't want their doctor to listen empathetically when they share their flu symptoms?

Beyond the realm of recovery and medical care, listening to stories is an important part of legacy building. Recently our daughter Keri drove to South Carolina to visit her grandparents and introduce them to her infant son, Noah. Together, they spent hours perusing photo albums. Keri looked through photos and newspaper clippings about the early years of Steve's grandparents' ministry in Africa. She listened as my in-laws told stories of what it was like to travel across the Atlantic Ocean on a barge with two toddlers (one of them being Steve) to begin their ministry in Nigeria, what it was like to raise four boys in Africa, and how heartbreaking it was to leave their boys in boarding school.

Later, Keri reflected on how meaningful her visit was and how she now had a far greater understanding of the godly legacy that's been passed down to her. Here are her reflections on that visit:

When I visited Grandma and Grandpa, I felt overwhelmed by the rich heritage I've been given. Looking through their photo albums, I saw pictures of them as well as previous generations of Harlings serving the Lord on the mission field. I saw pictures of Great Grandpa and Great Grandma Harling along with their team heading to the mission field to minister to a cannibal tribe in Nigeria. They planted churches and schools, and along with their partners, had the Word put in their tribal language.

I began to understand the rich blessing of the legacy that's been passed down to me. Every one of Grandma and Grandpa's kids and grandkids are walking with Jesus. Wow! That really struck me!

Listening to their stories was such a treasure for me. Over coffee and cookies I heard stories of what life was like in Nigeria, and what it was like in the states for Grandpa when his parents placed him in boarding school. I heard about the challenges of raising young children in Africa, sending their own kids to boarding school, and what the power of a spaghetti dinner and frosted chocolate brownies could do for four boys!

Through listening to their stories, I saw their tenderness toward Jesus and their faithfulness to His call. I thank God that my son already has a rich heritage in Christ because of them.

Listening to stories is powerful, and it isn't a new idea. It came from God. In fact, if you read through the Gospels, you'll begin to realize how important the stories of others were to Jesus.

Jesus Honored the Stories of Others

One day when the crowd was pressing in all around Jesus, a ruler from the synagogue fell at His feet and begged Jesus to come to his house and heal his daughter. Jairus's little girl was extremely ill. There's nothing scarier than when your kids are sick. Jairus's daughter was not just battling a sore throat or the common cold. She was dying, and her daddy felt desperate. Who could blame him? His daughter was going to die unless Jesus came! When Jesus heard Jairus's story, He felt deep compassion and agreed to go to Jairus's house.

But in the large crowd that day there was another desperate person. She had been bleeding for twelve years. According to Old Testament law, a woman was considered "unclean" for seven days after her monthly period (Leviticus 15:19–33). This poor woman had been considered unclean for twelve years! A person considered unclean at the time of Jesus could not enter the synagogue or even be touched by another human being. Can you imagine not being touched for over twelve years?

To make matters worse, she had spent all her money and had suffered a great deal under the care of doctors. According to the Talmud, which was an old Jewish document from the time of Jesus, there were eleven different cures suggested to treat women with the condition of continually bleeding. Some of the remedies suggested were tonics and astringents. One was to carry the ashes of an ostrich egg in a linen bag in the summer and in a cotton bag in the winter. Another was to carry a barley corn found in the dung of a white she ass.[2] Ladies, aren't you glad for hormone replacement therapy?! Feel free to give that a hearty *Amen!*

She had likely grown up hearing stories about the coming Messiah. When He came, He would "rise with healing" (Malachi 4:2 ESV). Cautiously, she followed from behind, and when she got just close enough, she reached out with desperation and touched the hem of Jesus' robe. Instantly, her blood flow stopped.

Jesus felt the power leave His body and turned to the crowd, asking, "Who touched me?" Make no mistake. Jesus knew. But Jesus also understood the need the woman had to process her story. When she realized there was no escape, she came trembling with fear, fell at His feet, and told Him her whole story (Mark 5:1–33).

It strikes me that Jesus took the time to let the woman to pour out her whole story! He didn't rush her or prompt her with hand motions to hurry up to get to the point. He simply listened as her story spilled out in brokenness. Imagine the anxiety that grew in Jairus as he waited. Meanwhile, a servant came running from Jairus's house to announce that his daughter had died. Reading the panic on Jairus's face, Jesus spoke calmly, "Don't be afraid, just believe" (Mark 5:36). If you finish reading the passage, you'll discover that Jesus continued to Jairus's home and brought his daughter back to life (Mark 5:40–42).

What Jesus modeled here for us as listeners is profound. He took the time for the woman to pour out her whole story. He gave the woman an opportunity to process all the pain and isolation she had felt over the last twelve years. What a gift!

The Key to Understanding

Relational wisdom from Proverbs teaches that if you want to understand others and deepen your relationship with them, you need to learn the art of drawing out their stories. "The purposes of a person's heart are deep waters, but one who has insight draws them out" (Proverbs 20:5). Imagine for a moment that you are wandering through a desert and are very thirsty. You're about to give up hope when you come across a well. You know that at the bottom of the well is fresh, clean water, but in order to get that water you have to use a bucket and draw it out. The bucket is sitting right there in the sand. What do you do? Of course, it's a no-brainer. You start lowering the bucket to draw out some water, right? You'd be foolish not to. The same principle applies in your relationships. If you're thirsty for deeper connection with your spouse, your kids, your friends, or your co-workers, start drawing out their stories. I promise you, you'll gain insight and discover deeper connection. But you have to be intentional or it won't happen. One method that I have found helpful is the "15-minute rule."

The 15-Minute Rule

When Steve and I were raising our family, we learned quickly that life with four kids was chaotic. Between sports, music lessons, and church activities, there was very little time left to connect as a couple, so we put into practice the "15-minute rule." It wasn't a hard-and-fast rule, but more of a guideline. Here's how it worked. For the first fifteen minutes when Steve got home from work, after he greeted the kids, we would retreat to a quiet space and tell each other the stories of our day. The kids knew they couldn't interrupt us unless there was an emergency. In those fifteen minutes, I learned to listen to my husband's heart. I had to learn to keep my focus on drawing him out and not trying to "fix." And truthfully, I didn't always do it right. Sometimes, for example, if a staff member was disrespectful, I felt myself getting defensive of my husband and would quickly suggest that Steve should fire that person. Not wise, but hey, I'm just keeping it real! Anyway, gradually, I learned to empathize with my husband without giving him suggestions for how to handle his job. Note the word *gradually*.

Learning how to draw out someone's story effectively is a process and develops over time. Your ability improves with practice. In a minute I'm going to give you specific tips for how to draw out someone's story, but first understand that if you make mistakes along the way, it's not the end. Just learn from your mistakes and ask God to help you grow in your ability to learn. The key is to be intentional and to use the 15-minute rule as a guide. The great thing is that the 15-minute rule can be used in lots of contexts.

Use the 15-minute rule with your kids when they get home from school or sports. Often, once they get wrapped up in homework, it can be a lost cause. Draw out the story of their day. Who did they sit by at lunch? Which teachers did they enjoy, and which annoyed them? What was the most enjoyable part of their day, and what part was most frustrating? Ask them fun questions to draw them out. Don't just ask about homework or they'll shut down faster than you can imagine.

The 15-minute rule also works well in the workplace. Before my daughter got married, she worked for a few years in a financial company. When she was first hired, her boss challenged her to conduct 15-minute interviews with every employee who worked for the company. She was instructed to visit with each employee and ask them to tell her their story. Bethany's first several weeks were focused very little on finances and much more on getting to know her co-workers. Clearly, that company valued community and caring for their employees. That's probably one of the reasons they are so successful!

After you've decided to become intentional and use the 15-minute rule, you might be wondering *how*. What are the most effective methods to draw out another person's story?

How?

In many ways, it's an art form to draw out a person's story, but there are a few key principles that you can put into practice right away. Each of these principles are easy to understand. They may feel awkward at first, but after you practice them a few times, you'll find them pretty simple, and listening to the stories of others will become enjoyable.

Resist the Urge to Dive In with Your Own Story

It's so natural! You're in a conversation with a co-worker who is sharing with you that they've just returned from a vacation in Costa Rica. How amazing! You've just been there yourself. What a coincidence! It's so tempting to dive in and tell her all about your recent vacation, the restaurants you visited, the hiking you did, and the zip lines you rode. But don't do it.

Whenever you dive in with your own story, you are stealing the microphone from the person who is telling their story. It reminds me of when one of my daughters was four. She and a friend were going to sing a duet in church. The friend was instructed to hold the microphone. But Bethany knew this was her moment to be a shining star. All through that little duet I watched my precious, sweet four-year-old try to steal the microphone from her friend. I was truly fearful that a fight would break out on stage! While that story still makes me smile, it's not funny when adults steal the mic.

The best advice is to remember to let someone be the star of their own show. Keep the focus on the person talking. This is an important skill for small group leaders. Often in a small group there is a time when participants are encouraged to share prayer requests. What often happens is that when people hear someone share their prayer request, they feel the urge to relate. For example, someone in the group may share that they need prayer for an upcoming interview. A person in the group dives in, saying, "Oh, the last time I went for an interview I felt so nervous, so I blah, blah, blah . . ." You get the point. The intentions were good, but without realizing it, the person trying to relate stole the mic. If you're a small group leader, help keep the group safe by reminding the group at the beginning of prayer request time that you'd like to have everyone feel comfortable sharing their requests, so if everyone will refrain from giving advice and keep relating to a minimum, everyone will hopefully feel safe to share.

Invite the Person to Tell You More

The principle of "tell me more" is to invite the other person to keep going with their story. You might say, "Tell me more," or ask, "And then what happened?" or "How did that make you feel?"

You can also use nonverbal signals like nodding your head, keeping eye contact, or smiling to encourage the other person to keep talking. We'll talk more about nonverbal signals in chapter 7, but for now, another way to invite them to tell you more is to lean slightly toward them. Not in a creepy way, just in an "I'm interested" kind of way.

Remember the Story

When you remember a person's story, you are saying that you value both the person and the relationship. Recently I was with a friend whom I hadn't seen for a couple of years. When we were together, I asked her how the Bible study she started in her home was going. She was shocked that I remembered and commented on what a great memory I had. Lest you get the wrong impression, I don't have a great memory! I was simply intrigued by the method she used to start a neighborhood Bible study after moving into a new community. I was genuinely interested. As I reflect back, I realize that's the key—I have to be genuinely interested. I have to ask the Holy Spirit to cultivate that in me as a wife, mom, friend, and speaker. I also realize I must give myself grace. When I'm speaking at an event and praying over lots of women and hearing lots of stories, it won't be realistic for me to remember everyone's story. I can't manage all those relationships. But for my close relationships, clients, and colleagues, I can't afford not to remember their stories, because stories matter.

Greg and Julie

I want to close this chapter with my friends Greg and Julie. Their stories were riddled with childhood abuse, a kidnapping, divorce, alcoholism, and shame. All of the baggage from their childhoods resulted in distrust, insecurity, and anger issues in their first years of marriage. After a few years of continual arguments, disagreements, and quarrels, something had to change. Julie decided to shift. She stopped talking and started listening. She asked more questions about Greg's childhood. She drew out the story of his first marriage. She sought to understand instead of demanding to be understood. She determined to stop trying to fix Greg and instead attempted to comprehend who Greg was and why. She gave up playing the Holy Spirit in Greg's life and instead offered unconditional love . . . and the results were phenomenal. Greg and Julie now have a thriving marriage. In fact, they speak all over the country on marriage and have written a book called *Two Are Better Than One*.

In your life, think about the people who matter most to you. It could be your spouse, a child, a co-worker, or a friend. How well do you know their story? How did their story influence the person they have become today and your relationship? Is it possible that you, like Julie, need to shift your focus to stop fixing and start understanding that person's story? If so, I've got great news for you. In the next chapter we'll be talking about silencing our inner fixer.

Listening to God

Try the 15-minute rule in your relationship with God. Set aside fifteen minutes every day to spend listening to God. Jesus said, "My sheep listen to my voice" (John 10: 27). That tells me that God wants us to set aside time to listen attentively to His voice. One of the ways we listen to the voice of God is by reading His Word and reflecting on what it speaks to us personally. Over the next few days, set aside fifteen minutes each day to read the Bible. If you haven't done this before, my recommendation is that you begin by reading the book of Mark or John. Both are found in the New Testament and are filled with stories of Jesus. I think you'll find them intriguing! As you read, ask God to speak to you. He loves to communicate! Each day write down one thing you feel He might have spoken to you, and then ask Him to affirm that thought. If you want more material on how to listen to God, you can go to my website, www.beckyharling.com, and download the free gift called "Listening to God."

Listening to Your Heart

1. On a scale of 1–10, 1 meaning hardly at all and 10 meaning very much so, how addicted to hurry are you? How does a sense of hurry prevent you from taking the time to listen

attentively to the stories of others? What would have to change for you to slow down? Journal your answers.

2. What is your story? Understanding your story can help you listen more attentively to the stories of others. Take fifteen minutes and create a timeline of your life. Mark the pivotal points that you felt were life-changing. Where was God during those moments of your life? Take some time and write out your story. Where have you seen evidence of God's goodness and faithfulness? This is for your benefit, so you don't need to worry if it's grammatically correct or well written. The purpose is to reflect on the faithfulness of God in your life story.

3. Can you think of a time recently when you stole the mic from someone else when they were trying to tell a story? Journal your answer. What could you do differently next time to encourage them to keep going and tell you more?

Listening to Others

Explore the story of your heritage. Take some time to interview and listen to the stories of your parents and grandparents. Ask about their childhood, time spent in the military, favorite holidays, traumas, trials, hopes, dreams, and faith. Then spend some time processing what you discovered. How have those stories impacted your heart? How has your heritage impacted your faith? How might their stories impact the legacy you'd like to leave?

Try the 15-Minute Rule

- Try the 15-minute rule at work or church by intentionally setting aside fifteen minutes to ask a co-worker or co-worshiper about their story. You could ask where they grew up, how many siblings they have, what brought them to the company or church, or any other question to draw out their story. Ask the Holy Spirit to help you stay interested as they talk. Resist the urge to steal the mic and dive in with your own story.

- Or you could try the 15-minute rule with your spouse or a close friend. Invite him or her to tell you the story of their day. Listen attentively and continue to draw him or her out. Use the phrase "Tell me more." Discipline yourself to wait until the person asks before you launch into the highs and lows of your day.

- Try the 15-minute rule with your kids. Take the first fifteen minutes after school or sports and see how much you can find out about your child's day.

4

Silence Your Inner Fixer

Never miss a good chance to shut up.

—Will Rogers

One TV show that I enjoy is *Fixer Upper* on HGTV. In case you're unfamiliar, the reality show features Chip and Joanna Gaines, who own and operate Magnolia Homes, a remodeling and design business in Waco, Texas. Chip and Joanna take viewers through the process of turning dilapidated houses into beautiful homes. Joanna's creative solutions are stunning. When I'm watching the show, I think to myself, *Joanna and Chip could solve all my decorating problems!*

The concept of fixing up old, run-down houses is brilliant, but trying to fix people? That's another story. What do I mean? Many of us wrestle with a fix-it mentality. A friend or spouse confides in us, and we've got just the creative solution. We know exactly what to do. As I'm writing this, I'm thinking about the well-meaning people who have tried to fix my problems.

I was speaking at a leadership conference where, afterward, a woman in the audience came up and said to me, "I can fix those dark circles under your eyes." Um, I don't remember asking for help on that.

Another time, a lady in the audience selling supplements told me she had just the solution to my energy problem. I just needed to buy her supplements. The thing is, I didn't even mention having an energy problem.

I'm certainly not the only recipient of unsolicited fixing. Parenting advice seems to abound for every mother of young children.

My daughter Keri was at a party when a woman she had never met before came up to her and asked if her son was sleeping through the night. Keri barely got the word *no* out of her mouth when the lady dove in with advice on exactly how to do it.

My friend Kimber told me that after she had her third child, a stranger came up and told her she could help her lose her belly fat with a magical wrap she was selling. Wow. Just, wow.

My daughter Bethany was in the grocery store, pregnant with her first child, when a man she had never met before came up to her and gave her a complete lecture on how to handle diaper rashes. The baby wasn't even out of her womb yet! I get a chuckle out of that story.

Ah yes. It seems that somewhere tucked down in our human nature is the desire to fix other people's problems. I recently asked my friends on Facebook if they had ever received unsolicited advice. I was hoping for a few good answers to prompt my thinking for this chapter. But I received well over fifty comments filled with stories where others had dumped their expertise uninvited. Apparently, unsolicited fixing is a bigger problem than most of us have realized. One story in particular stuck out to me.

Eileen had four miscarriages. Each time she miscarried, a fellow church member told her she needed to repent of sin in her life. Can you imagine? On top of all the grief a miscarriage brings, to have others dumping guilt left Eileen feeling hopeless. She repented of every sin she could think of. After a few years, she and her husband decided to adopt a sweet two-day-old infant. An older, supposedly wiser, Christian advised them, "Oh, you don't want to adopt. You don't know what demons this child is bringing!" What?! God's heart must break when His people say foolish things like that, especially since adoption is near and dear to His heart.

How is it that we who have problems ourselves are so quick to try to fix someone else's problem? James was spot on when he wrote, "Everyone should be quick to listen, slow to speak" (James 1:19). I'd like to suggest that a great paraphrase for this verse is, "Let everyone be quick to listen and slow to give advice!"

Lest I come across as innocent, I've dished out my fair share of unsolicited advice as well. There have been times, particularly with my adult kids, when a problem has been shared and I've jumped in with, "Why don't you try this?" or "You should do that!" Groan. Likely you have as well. Maybe your BFF opened up about a problem and internally you put on your fix-it hat and told her Exactly. What. To. Do.

Solomon wrote, "Answering before listening is both stupid and rude" (Proverbs 18:13 *The Message*). Ouch! When we give unsolicited advice and try to fix other people's problems, we're acting foolishly.

Remember Job's friends?

A Compelling Reason to Get Better Friends

In case you're unfamiliar with the story of Job, it's about a man whom God allowed Satan to test. As a result of the testing, Job lost everything. His kids. His home. His health. His wealth. After experiencing all that loss, Job's grief felt overwhelming. Devastated, he sat in the depths of despair.

Job's friends came at once to comfort him. For the first seven days they did awesome. They simply sat with Job. They offered their presence and the gift of silence. But after seven days, the need to fix kicked in, and Job's friends started dumping their solutions to Job's problems. "You must have sinned. Confess your sins and it will all be good. Don't be uptight about God's discipline. Maybe your kids did something wrong and that's why they died" (see Job 2–26). From that perspective, they attempt to fix Job's situation by telling him what to do. As I have studied this story, I believe Job's friends were trying to step into the role of mediator for Job, telling him how to navigate his relationship with God. But there is only one mediator in our relationship with God. His name is Jesus (1 Timothy 2:5).

Job's friends saw his situation from a human perspective. They felt bad for their friend and the pain he was suffering, but they had no idea about the heavenly perspective. They were unaware of the conversation that had happened in heaven between Satan and God. In essence, God felt so proud of Job that He allowed Satan to test him because He felt sure Job would stand firm in his faith.

We look at Job's friends and shudder. But is it possible that at times we've done the very same thing? A friend confides that she's having difficulty with her kids. Our fix-it mentality kicks in, and without another thought we dive in with all our knowledge. Or a co-worker complains about a rub in her marriage. We know just the book that will fix all her marriage problems. Bam! Without thinking, we clobber her with our "expertise." But in the process, we come across as condescending and bossy. With all our ideas, we imply that our friend doesn't have the wisdom to come up with her own solution.

We mean well. We don't want others to suffer pain. We want to fix things for them. Our love for Jesus compels us to change the world. But here's the thing: It's not to be a militant takeover by means of bossiness, but rather an organic movement of people coming to Christ because they are drawn to His love in us.

The irony is that the sharpest rebuke Jesus ever gave to any of His disciples was given to Peter, who had a knack for giving Jesus unsolicited advice and trying to fix Jesus' problems.

Jesus knew His death and resurrection was quickly approaching and began to prepare His disciples for the events that were about to happen. Peter, bless his heart, wanting to dive in to save Jesus, pulled Jesus aside and rebuked Him, advising Him not to say those kinds of things (Matthew 16:21–22). Don't you love it? Peter is so like you and me, wanting to be the expert, wanting to help Jesus out, and wanting to fix Jesus' problem!

In a rare display of frustration with one of His disciples, Jesus turned to Peter and said, "Get behind me, Satan! You are a stumbling block to me" (Matthew 16:23). Ouch! I wonder what went through Peter's mind at this point.

Peter was a slow learner, and a few days later he was right back at trying to fix things for Jesus. This time Jesus had taken Peter, James, and John to the top of a mountain. There on the mountaintop Jesus was transfigured before them. Sunlight poured from His face, and His clothes turned sparkling white. Moses and Elijah appeared, and once again Peter dove in with an idea! He advised, "Master, this is a great moment! What would you think if I built three memorials here on the mountain—one for you, one for Moses, one for Elijah?" (Matthew 17:4 The Message). This time, God the Father rebuked Peter. Out of heaven thundered a voice, "This is my Son, whom I love; with him I am well pleased. Listen to him!" (Matthew 17:5).

I gotta be honest. This passage convicts me to the core! I see a lot of me in Peter. I'm an idea person. In fact, according to StrengthsFinders,[1] "ideation" is one of my top leadership strengths. When I read the story of Peter and all his ideas, I am reminded that Jesus wants me to listen to others and go very slow with my ideas. Ouch! The same holds true for you.

What if the next time we launched into expert fix-it mode, God's voice boomed from heaven with, "This is my child whom I love; listen to her!" Or if the next time we tried to give advice to our husbands, we heard, "This is my beloved son; listen to him!" That might put the pause in our fix-it mentality.

Let's revise our paraphrase of James 1:19: "Each of us should be quick to listen and slow to fix someone else's problem."

Be Quick to Listen and Slow to Fix

Judging from the response on Facebook and private conversations I've had since then, many of us get this backward. We're quick to fix and slow to listen. James' warning is compelling. Here are five great reasons to *slow down* and *listen* before you dive in to fix:

1. You have enough to worry about in your own life. Who doesn't have problems? I'm guessing you, like me, have plenty. Being quick to solve another's problem can be a great way to run from your own problems. Instead, why not shift your focus. Focus your inner fixer on your own difficulties and your listening ear on others'. Most of the time, when a person confides in you about a problem they're experiencing, they just want someone to listen and confirm that what they're experiencing is difficult.

2. Your information might be incomplete. No matter what the situation is, it's impossible to know every detail of the problem the person is facing. For that reason, your quick solution would be incomplete. When you slow down and listen attentively, you can draw out more information about the problem.

Veronica received incomplete advice about her weight from several well-meaning friends at the church she attended. (Why anyone would advise another about weight is beyond me! Weight is such a personal issue!) Veronica's well-meaning friends noticed that she had gained some weight. In an effort to fix her "problem," they began suggesting diets, exercise programs, and all manner of supplements. The only problem? They didn't understand the issues because they hadn't spent time listening. Veronica's weight gain was due to a drug she had to use for cancer treatments. It had nothing to do with her eating habits. Only her doctor had the complete history and was able to help Veronica develop a weight management plan.

After reading Veronica's story, I would like to suggest that we each worry about our own weight and skip giving other people advice about theirs. Unless you're a doctor or a personal trainer, zip it and simply listen.

3. You'll come across as judgmental or condescending. Jesus' words were clear: "Do not judge, or you too will be judged" (Matthew 7:1). Unsolicited advice usually implies a person is doing something wrong and needs to be corrected. When we dish out unsolicited advice, we're judging the other person's ability to solve his or her own problem. As a result, we come off as condescending.

I don't like to feel like someone is patronizing me, do you? The truth is that I've come across that way to others when I've told them how to handle their problems. Lately, I've been praying, *Lord, please change me and uproot the tendency I have to come across as bossy or judgmental.* Friend, I would encourage you to pray that as well. I realize that for both you and me, change may take a lifetime, but I know the Holy Spirit will help both of us.

4. You'll be guilty of demeaning the person receiving your advice. Most problems are complicated. Rarely is there one solution. If you think you can solve someone else's problem in a few minutes, that implies the other person is an idiot. Dale Carnegie wrote that the greatest urge in the world is the desire to feel important.[2] We all want to feel significant. Rather than demeaning someone with your advice, why not bolster their confidence by assuring them that no one is more equipped to solve their problem than they are?

5. You're not God. The most profound reason I can think of to slow down and not offer a quick fix to someone's problem is because you're not God. That was the problem with Job's friends. They tried to play God in Job's life, when in reality they didn't have a clue what God's plan for Job's suffering was.

Your motives might be pure. You love the person and you hate to see them in pain. I get that. What brings out the fixer in me the quickest is when I sense that a loved one is discouraged. Automatically, my spirit wants to dive in and solve whatever is the cause of discouragement. I want those I love to feel happy. This is particularly true with my husband and kids.

Years ago, one of our daughters was walking through some deep waters of discouragement. Everything in me wanted to put on my mom fixer hat and change the situation for her. I felt helpless. I prayed. I wept. I processed my feelings with Steve. And then the Lord spoke to my heart. He reminded me that I'm not God. No kidding! I couldn't protect my child from Him. I couldn't protect my daughter from the refining He wanted to do in her life. Gently but firmly, the Holy Spirit invited me to open my hands and surrender my daughter to His plans. In my spirit, I heard the words, "I will fight for you while you remain silent." Those words came straight out of Scripture (Exodus 14:14), so I knew they were from the Lord. He invited me to remain silent except to praise Him that His plans for my child were *good* even though I couldn't see that at the time. Trust me, it was tough, but I'm so glad that I obeyed, because the work that God did in that child's life was beyond what I could have imagined.

Friend, if you struggle like me when your loved ones are hurting and you feel tempted to dive in and save them from pain, remind yourself that you're not God. He is at work. You may not see His plan, but He hasn't stepped off the throne. Praise Him that His plan is good. Then ask Him to help you to shift your focus from fixing to listening.

Now you might be wondering, *Well, Becky, what about the person I'm mentoring or discipling? Aren't I supposed to give them instruction and advice?* Here's my advice (LOL): Go slowly.

A Word About Mentoring Relationships

Mentoring both in the church and in the business community is growing. The idea behind a mentoring relationship is that someone who has already accomplished or arrived where you want to be walks alongside you to help you get where you want to go. As far as our spiritual journeys, Jesus said we are to disciple others. In other words, we are to walk alongside others, pointing them toward a deeper walk with God. Does this mean we give lots of advice? I don't believe so.

In my experience, the most effective mentors both professionally and spiritually listen attentively. They guide the conversation by asking great questions, modeling their walk with Christ, and offering their full, attentive presence to the mentee. Conference speaker Win Couchman has been known to say, "Mentoring works very nicely over a cup of coffee."[3] I love that statement, not only because I love a good cup of Starbucks, but because it speaks to the organic, friendly nature of mentoring. It's not a teaching session. It's more of a journey through life together with one person taking the lead and another being willing to follow.

I had the distinct privilege of being mentored by author and speaker Linda Dillow. When we were together, I asked Linda as many questions about her walk with God, her ministry, her writing, and her speaking as I could think of. We prayed together, laughed together, and cried together. When I needed to process frustrations in ministry, Linda listened. When I felt like a failure, Linda encouraged. By the way, Linda is still in my life. We talk as often as we can by phone, we pray together, and we see each other as often as possible. Her ongoing presence in my life is a gift I don't take lightly. As a result, I have been able to pass that gift on to others.

As a mentor I often invite, "Ask me anything. I am an open book." I answer questions, but I also ask questions pertaining to how the mentee's marriage is doing, or how she is feeling in the realm of parenting, or how she is spending time nurturing her walk with God. When I feel tempted to give advice, I pause and pray and ask the Holy Spirit to help me remember that I am not to be a fixer in the person's life. If there is blatant sin, I will bring it to the person's attention and ask her if she's considered the impact that sin might have on her life. I point out sin, but I also realize I can't make a choice for others. I am to be merely a gentle guide, walking alongside and allowing my life to point her to Jesus. When I feel tempted to fix, I purposefully shift my focus.

Is a Confrontation the Same as Advice?

On rare occasions, you might need to confront. That's different from offering advice on solving a problem. A confrontation is a face-to-face meeting where you bring a problem to light in order to find a solution. For example, Janae blew the whistle and confronted a preschool teacher when she realized the teacher was crossing the lines of discipline and abusing the children. The abuse needed to be addressed and reported for the safety of the children. Janae bravely confronted the teacher and the school supervisor, and in the end, the teacher was fired.

The principle to remember here is that a confrontation is different from diving in with your advice to fix someone's problem. In a case like the one above, you're not offering suggestions, you're giving them the solution.

When You're Tempted to Fix, Shift Your Focus

Focus on Following the Golden Rule

When you're listening to someone who is sharing a problem with you, or complaining about a situation they're facing, listen to them in a way you would want them to listen to you. It's the golden rule of listening (Luke 6:31). Rather than asserting yourself as the one with the answer, position yourself as a friend who is seeking to understand. A few chapters later, we'll be talking about empathy and the best ways to validate and help another feel understood. But in the meantime, listen with an understanding heart the way you would want someone to listen to you.

Focus on Offering Dignity and Honor

Most people struggle with some type of insecurity. Many feel like failures. The last thing a person needs is to have you validate those feelings in them by dumping a ton of advice on them. Instead, dignify them by agreeing that the situation they are facing is tough. Focus on making them feel important. Tell them you admire them for being brave enough to face their problem head on. Affirm them for seeking God or wanting support or anything else you can think of. Jesus offered dignity and worth to every person, even those who had made terrible mistakes in their lives.

Focus on Listening to Find Feelings

Instead of trying to come up with a solution, shift your focus to listening for feelings. Is the person feeling unloved or like a failure? Overwhelmed? Lonely? Discouraged? If you're not sure what's being felt, ask. You might say, "It sounds like you're feeling discouraged. Am I right?"

Ask yourself, *How is this difficulty impacting the other person's life? Is it leaving the person exhausted, depressed, or simply paralyzed?* Then ask specifically, "What can I do to help?"

My kids are all married and raising kids. Each family has a baby in the mix. When one of my daughters calls me and says, "Wow, I'm tired. The baby didn't sleep at all last night. This kid never sleeps," the best thing I can do in that moment is say, "Oh sweetie, I'm sorry. That sounds discouraging and exhausting! You're such a great mama; you're so patient." That way I offer sympathy and also encouragement. If, on the other hand I say, "Oh, well let me tell you, here's what you need to do. . . ." and then go off on a three-part plan to get a baby to sleep through the night, I can tell you, my girls would hang up. They don't want my advice in that moment. They want empathy and perhaps an offer to baby-sit!

What's ironic is when I commiserate with my girls and affirm them, they'll often ask, "Mom, what did you do? When did we sleep through the night?" To which I reply, "Some of you slept through the night from two months; others not until you moved out and went off to college." If my girls tell me they are asking for advice, I will give it—but *very* cautiously. I might offer them options, and I try to use language that implies there's not only one way to do things.

Those of us who are mothers to adult kids must be careful not to come across as the expert. Experts intimidate. You don't want your kids intimidated by you. You want them to feel like they can approach you with any problem. In light of that, ask the Lord to put His almighty hand over your mouth. You might help Him out by buying some duct tape! Your kids will back way up and not want to hang with you if they sense you're going to give them advice. If they want your advice, they'll ask. In the meantime, clarify what they're feeling, empathize, and affirm. I've found with our kids, no matter how old they get and how successful they are, a little affirmation goes a long way. As their mom, I would far rather err on the side of affirming them too much than on the side of offering too much advice. But even though I know that, I still slip sometimes. When I do, I try to apologize quickly.

Similarly, with your friends, listen for feelings and the chance to offer affirmation. Seek to validate. Don't try to fix! Simply offer your listening presence.

Tanya wrote me that after confiding in a friend that she had been traumatized as a child because of sexual abuse, her friend reached across the table, grabbed Tanya's hand, and then said, "Do yourself a favor, just move on!" Oh my. Jesus *never* told anyone to just get over it. Tanya felt devastated that her friend didn't understand the toll sexual abuse had taken on her body, soul, and spirit.

Recently, Steve was at a meeting with executives from around the state. As a group, they were working on their listening skills as leaders. Everyone in the room was given a red card and a green card. A person at each table shared a problem. Those around the table were to listen and empathize but not fix. If a person offered advice, the other CEOs around the table were to hold up a red card. After a time of listening, the CEOs were allowed to ask each other, "Where do you think God is in this?" And, "Are there any Scripture verses that might apply?" Steve's experience led me to my next suggestion.

Focus on Asking a Question

When I feel tempted to give advice, I've learned to ask a question. The three questions below have often helped me to shift my focus. They keep the other person talking, and they help keep me focused on listening instead of fixing.

- **Where do you see God in this problem?** This is a great question all around because it gives you insight into how to pray for your friend. Some people visualize God far away and out of touch with their problem. Others may view Him up close and weeping with them in their problem. Still others may feel He is trying to teach them a lesson. Always ask them how they view God in their problem.

- **Is God speaking anything to you?** I also love this question because it implies that people can hear from God. God wants to communicate, so I often ask this question, particularly when I am listening to someone who is a faith-filled person.

- **What do you think you might do?** Often a person has several options already in mind for solving their problem, but they are looking for someone to process their options with. Don't offer a solution, but do ask what options they have. This also helps people realize that they do have options. We always have options when solving a problem, and this question can serve as a gentle, non-advice reminder.

In the next chapter we're going to talk more about asking great questions, so hang with me and keep reading. Learning to ask questions will enhance your listening skills and restrain your desire to fix another's problem. And the great news is, it's an easy skill to implement.

If it all feels a bit overwhelming, don't stress. You're making progress, and you're not always going to get it right. Neither am I. When we blow it and dive into fix-it mode, the best idea is to simply confess quickly. Pray, *Lord, I blew it. Would you set a guard over my mouth? When I feel tempted to fix, remind me to affirm or ask a question instead. Help me to stay on the journey of learning to listen so that those I'm in relationship with feel valued and honored.*

Listening to God

1. Read John 16:12. Jesus said He had more to say to us. How does our constant need to fill silence prohibit us from hearing God's voice? When we sit in silence before God, we don't conjure up new solutions to our problems. We simply sit and wait for Him to speak.

2. Read Revelation 8:1. How might becoming more comfortable with silence help curb your fixing tendencies?

3. Practice sitting in silence with God for five minutes. During the five minutes, practice sitting still and just listening. Try not to think through your to-do list or come up with solutions to problems. Simply sit and be present to God. Then write down what you experienced.

4. Listen to "On The Throne" by New Life Worship.[4] As you listen, praise God that He is on the throne. Because He is sovereign, He is able to help your loved ones solve their problems, so you don't need to dive in as the fixer. As you listen, if you feel that God speaks anything to your spirit, write it down.

Listening to Your Heart

Create some space in your schedule and, if at all possible, go to a private place to reflect on these questions. Begin by asking God to search your heart once again and show you what is driving you to be the advice giver.

5. Think back to a recent time when you gave someone some unsolicited advice. What were you hoping for out of that situation?

6. In what ways does being viewed as the expert build your self-esteem?

7. Often when a person we love is experiencing a significant problem, we feel helpless. Journal about a time when a loved one was experiencing loss or anxiety and you felt helpless. How did God meet that person? What good came out of your helplessness?

8. Write a prayer to the Lord, confessing any tendency you have to try to fix. Then ask the Lord to uproot that tendency in you and replace it with a deeper desire to listen.

Listening to Others

9. Think back to a recent time when you gave someone unsolicited advice. Go back to that person and apologize. Ask them to forgive you and to help hold you accountable so that you don't repeat the same pattern.

10. Look for the opportunity to practice your skills. When someone shares a problem with you today, shift your focus from fixing to listening. Then affirm their ability to figure out a solution and ask them a question to keep them talking.

5

Ask Great Questions

Good leaders ask great questions that inspire others
to dream more, think more, learn more, do more, and
become more.

—John C. Maxwell

In one of my training sessions to become a certified leadership
coach, we were given a set of juggling balls and then paired up
with a partner. We were instructed to coach each other on how
to juggle the balls.

The first time we did the exercise, everyone in the room was
busy trying to give each other instructions and suggestions: "Try
throwing the balls a little higher. Try to get the rhythm. Focus.
You can do it!" You could hear lots of laughter around the room
as balls went flying through the air, but no one improved.

As we were scrambling to retrieve our juggling balls, our instructor asked us to describe how we felt when our partner was
giving lots of instructions. The majority of us answered, "Anxious,
stressed, and nervous."

Then our coaching instructor told us to repeat the exercise, but this time we were only allowed to ask questions. Around the room you could hear people asking, "How did that work?" "What do you think went wrong?" "What could you do differently next time?" "How did that feel?" The difference at the end of the second round was remarkable. Almost everyone in the room improved their juggling, and people felt more peaceful. Our instructor's point was clear. Don't tell people what to do; ask them questions.

When you ask questions, you turn your ear to wisdom and apply your heart to understanding (Proverbs 2:2). Not only do you grow in your understanding of a person, but often a great question prompts the person to greater understanding of themselves. You gain greater insight, they gain greater self-awareness, and the two of you grow closer. It's a relational win-win! This is why Jesus asked questions so often throughout His earthly ministry.

The Master of Great Questions

Jesus was the master of great questions. Ever noticed? Think about it. His style was conversational and approachable. He was, in essence, the greatest of all coaches. He understood and modeled life-giving questions: "What do you want me to do for you?" (Luke 18:41), "Do you believe that I am able to do this?" (Matthew 9:28), "Why are you so afraid?" (Matthew 8:26), "Do you love me?" (John 21:17), "Who do you say I am?" (Mark 8:29), "Do you want to get well?" (John 5:6).

My favorite out of those stories is the one with Jesus and the blind man.

As Jesus was approaching Jericho, a blind man sat by the side of the road begging. Those who were blind had an extremely hard time making a living. Most resorted to begging to earn enough money to eat. The man outside the gates of Jericho was no exception. He sat by the side of the road begging and listening intently for those who would pass by who might be able to spare some change. But on the day when Jesus was approaching Jericho, he heard something different in the air. Excitement. Anticipation. Expectation. As the crowd moved past him, he asked those around him, "Hey, what's going on?" Whatever it was, he sensed it was something extraordinary! People around him told him that Jesus of Nazareth was passing by. In that moment, the blind man saw his opportunity. It's safe to say he had heard about the miracles Jesus had done, because he started shouting from the side of the road, "Jesus, Son of David, have mercy on me!" Even when those around him told him to be quiet, he continued shouting. I love that this man took initiative and had the persistence to keep crying out even though others told him to shut up.

Jesus stopped, approached the blind man, and asked him a very simple question. It's so simple that it's almost shocking, but oh, so profound! "What do you want me to do for you?" (Luke 18:41). Have you ever wondered why Jesus asked this? I mean, wasn't it obvious what this man wanted? By asking that question, Jesus gave the man the opportunity to state what he wanted and what he felt his greatest need was.

What an incredible gift Jesus gave this man. How often people long to say what they want or what they need, but no one asks, so they remain silent. Wishing. Longing. Hoping. Jesus knew the desire of the blind man's heart, but out of deep love for him, He asked the question, giving him the opportunity to state his desire. Friend, when we dare to ask someone what they want, we give them the opportunity to verbalize their need, and the result is powerful.

Without hesitation, the blind man stated that he wanted to see. Jesus healed him, and instantly this blind man's life was changed forever.

Jesus asked questions that offered people the opportunity to reflect and reveal what was in their hearts. Every time Jesus asked a question, people had the opportunity to look inside. *What do I want? Why am I so afraid? Do I want to get healed? Who do I think Jesus is?* As a result, people didn't feel attacked by Jesus; they felt safe enough to answer. He was their friend. They felt comfortable expressing what they needed and wanted. As you think about your relationships, consider for a moment:

When was the last time you asked someone close to you a great question? Do you take time to ask your friends, neighbors, and co-workers questions? And if you do, what type of questions do you ask? The best questions allow people to explore what's in their hearts. When people feel heard, they walk away from a conversation thinking, *Wow, that was the greatest conversation!*

Wanna Be a Great Conversationalist?

What's the first thing that comes to your mind when you hear the word *conversation*? I'm guessing your first thought was talking. But guess what? Did you know that 80 percent of a successful conversation involves listening? In fact, take a moment and think back on the most fulfilling conversation you've had recently. You may have walked away thinking, *Wow, what a rich conversation!* That's when it dawned on you. The reason you felt it went so well is because you did all the talking and the other person listened! Great conversationalists all have one thing in common: They ask questions that draw others out. Why? Because they, like Jesus, understand the simple truth: People love to talk about themselves.

Author Sonya Hamlin writes, "Listening requires giving up our favorite human pastime—involvement in ourselves and our own self-interest. It's our primary, entirely human focus. And it's where our motivation to do anything comes from."[1] We're so very human, aren't we?

Whether we want to admit it or not, we love to talk about ourselves. I recently read an article that supports this truth. Harvard neuroscientists write, "It feels so rewarding, we *can't help* but share our thoughts. This makes sense when you realize that talking about our own beliefs and opinions, rather than those of other people, stimulates the meso-limbic dopamine system, which is associated with the motivation and reward feelings we get from food, money and sex."[2] Wow. If you needed scientific proof, there you have it.

I first learned this when I was a young teen and getting ready to go out on my first date. I had a serious case of the jitters! What was I going to talk about? A wise friend gave me great advice: "Don't worry at all about what to talk about. Boys love to talk about themselves. So just plan a few good questions and you won't have to think of a thing to say. Ask your date about his awards and accomplishments, and he'll just keep talking." Awesome. That little piece of advice saved my dating relationships and many other relationships to follow because it's true. People *do* love to talk about themselves. Honestly, if you enter every conversation with a few good questions, you'll always be viewed as an amazing conversationalist.

So when you're in a conversation, how do you remember to ask questions? Here's an easy trick I use: There are two Cs to great conversation—curiosity and connecting.

Stay Curious and Seek Connection

Stay Curious

Instead of letting your nerves drive you when you meet someone new, train yourself to stay curious. Play a little game with yourself. See how much you can find out about a person within the first ten minutes of a conversation.

You might ask: How long have you been coming to this church? Where do you live? Do you have children? Do you work outside the home? What's your favorite part of your job?

When you're in a tense conversation and you find your palms getting sweaty, remind yourself to stay curious. Try to figure out what the other person is feeling by asking questions rather than trying to change the other person's thinking. We'll talk about how to do this in the next section, but for now, remember, in every conversation, stay curious. And as you're working to stay curious, seek to stay connected by asking connecting questions.

Seek Connection

Think of it this way: Connecting questions are questions that help you build a bridge into another person's world. They'll help you find common ground. When you're trying to think of a question to ask, remind yourself, *I'm trying to connect.* That will help you come up with a question.

For example, my grandson Charlie just started school. My daughter Stefanie wanted to reach out to some of the other moms and form connections. So she began a conversation with a mom of another kindergartner, asking, "How is your son adjusting to kindergarten?" Immediately a bridge was built, and the two moms began to chat.

By reminding yourself of the two Cs, you'll be able to navigate almost any conversation smoothly. Others will feel comfortable with you, and you'll find you have greater impact and a wider circle of friends.

Using the principles of *curiosity* and *connecting*, let's take a look at five times when the stakes are too high for you not to ask a question!

Five Times It Will Benefit You to Ask a Question

When you're tempted to dive in with an idea or offer a solution

I know we just spent an entire chapter on not fixing other people's problems. But because this seems to be such a big issue for many of us, I think it bears repeating.

I remember a time in Steve's life when he was experiencing quite a few problems at the church where he worked. He often came home anxious and frustrated. During that season, when Steve arrived home, we went for a walk and he poured out his heart. Most days our walks went well. But I remember one day when there was not only tension because of Steve's work situation, there was also friction between us. And the problem was me. Groan.

Remember, as I shared in the last chapter, I'm an idea person. But sharing my brilliance when my husband was pouring out his heart was not my wisest choice. After a long pause following my brilliance, Steve said, "Beck, I don't want your advice. I only want you to listen." Ouch!

After that conversation I went before the Lord and asked Him what I needed to do to change. The answer I received was to learn how to ask questions to keep Steve talking. As a result, I began to study question asking. Now truthfully, I'm still growing in this area. I mean, it's just so tempting at times to dive in with the perfect idea. But I'm learning, ever so slowly, to ask a question instead. The truth is that people want to feel heard. They don't want you to solve their problems. Generally, they can figure things out themselves.

Steve also has had to learn this. Sometimes I have poured out my heart to him and he has seen the solution as clear as day and has tried to fix things for me. But it leaves both of us frustrated.

You might be thinking, *How do I come up with a question on the spot, Becky?* Look at you! You're already asking questions, and that's a great one, by the way.

Here's what's helped me. Look up some great questions and learn to use them well. Here are just a few of my favorites for situations when I feel tempted to dive in with an idea or offer a solution.

- Then what happened?
- How did you feel when he or she said that?
- How did others in the room react when that happened?
- What do you think you should do next?
- What does your spouse think? (I often ask this when my adult kids are sharing a problem with me because I want to do everything humanly possible to build up their marriages.)
- Is there anything I can do to help you?

• What do you need from me?

By having a few good questions in my head, it's easier not to fall back on old habits!

When you're trying to re-establish intimacy or closeness with someone

Every relationship experiences conflict. We'll talk about this more in chapter 8. Sometimes after conflict one person feels the need to pull back and put distance in the relationship. That can be healthy and even good, but it also might be the perfect time to ask a few great questions both of yourself and the other person. Let's start with you.

The first question you might ask yourself is, "How much do I value this relationship?" I always start here because drawing someone back into intimacy takes hard work, and I need to be sure I am prepared to do that work. And asking myself that question helps me put into perspective what's happening. If I value the relationship deeply, it motivates me to work on resolving the conflict no matter how great the cost. For example, if the conflict has been with my husband and I notice he's withdrawing, because I value that relationship immensely, I know I need to put the time and effort into re-establishing the lost intimacy. Similarly, with my adult kids or a close friend, I remind myself how deeply I value that relationship.

Moving forward, I take initiative and ask, "Are you doing okay?" Depending on the answer, I might continue, "Is there something I've done to upset you?" If I still sense distance but am not getting a clear response, I might wait and return to the subject later. Or I might move forward with, "It feels like there's some distance between us. Do you feel that way too? Do you feel up to exploring that with me?" These questions allow the other person to agree or disagree to resolving the conflict, or admit that they need more time and energy before re-establishing closeness.

Moms need to be careful with our tone as we ask these questions because one trap that we often fall into is guilting our kids! I don't know about your kids, but I sure know mine. And they don't respond well to guilt. When I ask, "Have I offended you?" it needs to be a genuine, no-strings-attached question! I need to have a completely open posture ready to receive the answer. My intent cannot be to manipulate them into giving me the answer they think I want to hear. Cultivating honest and open communication with my adult kids is something I deeply value.

Other great questions to use when trying to close the distance:

- I'd like to understand. Can you help me understand what you're feeling?
- It sounds like you feel tense. What did I say that made you feel that way?
- What do you need from me?

When you're meeting someone for the first time

I enjoy meeting new people. I love hearing their stories and details about their lives. Every person is intriguing and worth knowing. But not everyone enjoys meeting new people. For some, meeting someone new is a terrifying experience. If you get nervous meeting new people, prepare three questions to ask. If you go into every meeting prepared, you won't feel half as nervous, and you'll maybe even feel excited. And I promise you, your meeting will go a whole lot better!

You can always start with some basics:

- How long have you lived here?
- Do you have family in this area?
- What do you love most about your neighborhood? (This same question can be adapted to what a person loves most about their church, their job, their school, their state, or their country.)

- Where did you grow up? What was the culture like in your town as a kid?

You get the idea. The point is that there is a world full of people. Each one is valuable and unique and loved by God. So take the time to get to know them. If you feel nervous, learn the art of asking questions to draw the other person out.

When you feel confused or concerned

When we were raising our kids, one of them came home from school discouraged and lethargic. I could tell that something had happened during the day and that I was going to have to handle the situation gently because my child looked extremely defeated. I began with a snack. (Food always works when you're trying to get them to relax and talk, right?) Then I started by asking how school was. I got the standard reply: "Fine." I felt pretty sure things were not "fine" by looking at my child's face. I continued gently, "What was the highlight for you?"

"Lunch."

Ah, food does speak!

I asked a bit gingerly, "How was recess?"

"Fine."

"How did you do on your spelling test?"

"I got 100 plus 5," followed by tears.

I felt confused. Who cries over 105? I remember pausing and praying. And then I asked, "Is there something you want to tell me?" Ah, that's when I got the confession.

"I cheated."

I was pretty sure I had heard wrong. My son was smart. Tests were never a problem for him, and I couldn't imagine why he would cheat. But I paused, and he poured out his confession.

After he told me his story, we headed out the door and went back to school with an apology and lots of tears! That little event was life-changing for my son. He never cheated again.

When you're feeling confused or concerned, pause and then ask a question that might help you understand what's really going on. I've heard it said that every sentence has a history. Make it your goal to try to understand the history behind each sentence.

When you are leading a meeting

If you are in any kind of leadership role, whether you're leading a project at work, a committee at church, a neighborhood association, or the PTA at your child's school, learn to lead like Jesus and ask questions. This allows others to know you care about them and that you value their opinions.

In one of my early leadership roles I was the Director of Women's Ministries at a church. I felt nervous about how to best lead a meeting. My husband, Steve, taught me to start every meeting with a question. This did two things: It helped me get a glimpse into everyone's heart right from the beginning of the meeting, and it allowed those on my team to feel valued and heard. To this day, whenever I'm leading a meeting, I use a question within the first few minutes to draw others in. Again, it comes back to being a magnet to draw people to you rather than away from you.

The same principle holds true in a coaching relationship. Coaching is the art of learning to ask the right questions and then listening very attentively. The person being coached can find the answer within themselves. Whether you are a coach, a counselor, or someone who benefits from these services, remember that questions allow you to be on equal footing with each other, and you can share more freely together when a question is on the table.

It All Comes Back to Jesus

Friend, as we close this chapter, let's go back to Jesus. I want to be about everything related to Jesus, don't you? I want to love like Jesus, listen like Jesus, and lead like Jesus. If I am going to love, listen, and lead like He did, I have to become skilled at asking questions.

The same holds true for you. It's not that hard for us to ask meaningful questions. It just takes practice and intentionality. Why don't you start by praying this prayer:

Lord Jesus, I love you. I long to be transformed into a person who listens and loves others effectively just like you. Holy One, as I intentionally learn and practice asking questions, would you, through the power of your Holy Spirit, transform me into a person who listens attentively? Bring to my mind the questions that will help to draw others out so that they feel comfortable opening their heart to mine. When I feel tempted to focus on myself rather than others, bring conviction, I pray. Teach me what it looks like to shift my focus moment-by-moment so that the people I'm listening to feel like you yourself have been listening to them.

EXERCISES TO
Strengthen Your Ear

Listening to God

1. One of the most effective ways we prepare our hearts to listen to God is by spending time in worship and praise. As we praise God, He brings our spirit into union with His Spirit. In preparation to listen for God's voice, listen to "Spirit of the Living God" by Vertical Church.[3] As you listen, make the words the cry of your heart. Ask the Holy Spirit to quiet any voice other than His own so that you can hear what He is speaking to you.

2. Read John 21:15–19 once out loud, then read the passage at least two times slowly. Then sit silently and imagine Jesus sitting in the room with you, asking, "Do you love me?" Sit with that question silently for at least five minutes. How do you feel you want to respond to Jesus' question?

3. Think back over some of the questions Jesus asked. Which question is your favorite and why? How does the question speak to you personally?

4. Think back over the material you read in this chapter. Sit silently for five minutes. What do you think God is speaking to you from this chapter? What part of the chapter resonated with you the most?

Listening to Your Heart

5. What is the most profound question you have ever been asked?

6. Think back over conversations you've had recently. Have you become defensive in response to any question recently? What was the question that made you feel defensive? How did you respond? Could you have given a different response? What prevented you from responding differently? What would you change next time?

7. Is it easy or difficult for you to meet new people? Is there anything you could do to make it easier? How might asking questions help you in meeting new people?

8. What action step will you take moving forward?

Listening to Others

9. Think back to the last time you met someone new. How did you establish a connection? What questions did you ask?

10. Reflect back on the last conflict you had. Then answer the following questions:
    - Who was the conflict with?
    - How much do you value that relationship?
    - What questions did you ask during the conflict to stay curious?
    - What questions did you ask to help you understand the other person's perspective?
    - What could you do differently next time?

11. How might asking questions help shift your thinking from yourself to the other person?

12. Over the course of the next few days, have coffee with a friend or new acquaintance. Pre-plan three questions you will ask the other person.

13. Spend a few minutes thinking about your most challenging relationship. How might asking questions transform that relationship?

Transformational Questions

Questions When a Problem Feels Overwhelming

1. What's your greatest concern?

2. What obstacle is getting in the way?

3. Who else could possibly help you?

4. What would you tell a friend who was in this situation?

5. If that doesn't work, what's your backup plan?

6. What are the advantages of doing it that way?

7. What are the disadvantages of doing it that way?

8. What's working for you now?

9. What would you like to see change?

10. What would bring you the most satisfaction?

11. How will your decision impact your family?

12. What do you sense God is inviting you to do?

13. What practical step will you take to feel less overwhelmed?

Questions to Help Resolve a Conflict

1. I want to understand—can you help me understand your perspective?

2. What do you need from me?

3. What makes you think I feel that way?

4. What does that look like for you?

5. Where can we go from here?

6. What would you like to see happen?

Questions to Help You Get to Know Someone

1. What do you do for a living?

2. How long have you lived here?

3. Where did you grow up?

4. Do you have any children?

5. Where do your children attend school?

6. Do you have any extended family in the area?

7. What do you enjoy doing for fun and recreation?

8. What do you like most about your job?

9. Do you enjoy travel? What is your favorite place that you've been in the last year?

10. What jobs have you worked previously?

Questions to Begin a Meeting

1. What are you most excited about in our company?

2. What characteristics do you value most in a team member?

3. What's the greatest strength you bring to this team?

4. If you could change one thing about your job, what would that be?

5. When you've felt most successful at work, what factors were present?

6. What was one win you experienced last week?

7. How do we know as a team when we've done a great job?

8. What new skill have you learned in the last month?

9. If you could learn one new skill to make you more effective at your job, what would it be?

10. Have you seen any member of our team go above and beyond the call of duty recently? If so, what did they do?

These questions are merely a springboard for you to launch into your own conversations, which is the real goal of what we've been talking about in this chapter. It doesn't take much to ask great questions, but it does take being intentional.

I had a group of friends help me develop the list of questions. One of the women in the group began using some of these questions in the coffee shop where she works, and the results were phenomenal. Instantly, co-workers began viewing her as their friend and started opening up. You can use the list of questions above and allow them to prompt you to think of your own questions!

Great questions can be used at small groups, networking events, church or school socials, and neighborhood gatherings, in addition to everyday settings. When used with the right motive, they can cultivate deeper intimacy in marriage. Friend, whether you're at a doctor appointment or a parent-teacher conference, meeting a new acquaintance or a dear friend, a business client or a potential employer, it's wise to have a few well-thought-out questions in your pocket.

Over the last few years I have used the time in driving to an appointment to prepare three questions in my mind. If I'm meeting a friend, I think back to the last time we were together and remember what we talked about then. I try to follow up with a question about whatever was going on in that person's life at the time. This intentional practice has helped my scattered brain stay much more focused on whoever I'm with. Gradually, I'm improving my listening skills, and I know that you can too! As you stay focused on asking great questions, make sure that you are aware of which questions bring the most positive response. Then the next time you can return to the same subject. Now, who are you going to ask first? Here's to successful conversations all the way around!

6

Offer Empathy, Validate Feelings

No one cares how much you know, until they know
how much you care.

—unknown

When Steve and I were raising our kids, we realized that we needed a theme verse to keep our family on track with the vision God had given us. The verses we landed on were found in Proverbs 24:3–4:

> By wisdom a house is built,
> and through understanding it is established;
> through knowledge its rooms are filled
> with rare and beautiful treasures.

We wanted each of our children to feel understood, valued, and loved. We knew that would take a lot of wisdom and knowledge. In our home, this meant laughing with our kids when they were silly, crying with them when they felt sad, cheering for them when they felt overwhelmed, and understanding them when they felt angry. As Steve and I studied the truths taught in Proverbs 24:3–4, we discovered they held great relational truth not just for our family but for our friendships and colleagues alike.

If we substituted the word *relationship* for *house*, the verses would read, "By wisdom a *relationship* is built and through understanding the *relationship* is established; through knowledge the *relationship* is filled with rare and beautiful treasures."

Our relationships definitely take wisdom and knowledge, but I want to focus in this chapter on the phrase, "Through understanding it is established." Our bonds are established and strengthened when understanding is offered. The image behind the Hebrew poetic language here paints the picture of something that has been toppled over being gently reestablished. It makes me think of all the lamps that got toppled over when we were raising our four active and energetic kids.

At times a person's emotions leave them feeling toppled over. In the chaos of sorrow, anger, anxiety, fear, or frustration, energy is depleted and exhaustion follows. What's needed is a friend or loved one to help them restabilize by offering understanding and empathy.

What Is Empathy?

If I were to define empathy, I would describe it as the ability to identify with another person's feelings and circumstances. It's like offering the other person the gift of understanding. Empathy goes beyond intellectual acknowledgment of a person's feelings to an emotional connection. It's the idea that the apostle Paul was getting at when he wrote, "Rejoice with those who rejoice; mourn with those who mourn" (Romans 12:15).

Empathy is the ability to put yourself in someone else's shoes so that you can understand their struggles. So when a friend is pouring out their heart to you, try to imagine what it would feel like to be in their situation.

Here's an exciting truth: God hardwired your brain to empathize with others because it is mutually beneficial for both the person offering empathy and the person receiving empathy. In fact, in the last decade, scientific research has uncovered the existence of "mirror neurons," which react to emotions expressed by others and then reproduce them.[1] The neurons are located in our brain and are wired to respond to the emotions of others so that we can mirror their feelings. In other words, science has confirmed how God created our brains—to connect empathetically with others. Don't you just love it when science confirms what Scripture teaches?

When you offer empathy, you not only help re-stabilize the person who feels toppled over, but you unlock the door to deeper connection and increase your sense of community. All of this makes sense because you were created in God's image and God is social. He values community. He exists in three persons, called the Trinity: God the Father, God the Son, and God the Holy Spirit. Within the Trinity there is deep fellowship and connection. He designed you in His image with a deep need for fellowship and community as well.

If you doubt this, just look at Jesus.

Jesus Was the Master of Empathy

Jesus didn't just imagine being in our shoes. He stepped into our humanity by becoming a baby. He grew up and dealt with people all the time. If you read through the gospel accounts of Jesus' life, you will discover that He consistently empathized with people and made them feel valued. "When he saw the crowds he had compassion" (Matthew 9:36). He said to the crowd that gathered on the hillside to hear Him preach, "Blessed are those who mourn" (Matthew 5:4). When Lazarus died, Jesus wept with Martha and Mary, Lazarus's sisters, because He felt empathy for them (John 11:36). When Jesus and His disciples were visiting the town of

Nain, Jesus saw a funeral procession. Scripture tells us that "His heart went out to" the widow of Nain because her only son had died. Now she was without husband or son. Jesus felt deeply moved by compassion when He saw the widow's plight and took action, raising the widow's son back to life (Luke 7:11–15).

Jesus consistently offered empathy and understanding. The writer of Hebrews wrote, "We do not have a high priest who is unable to empathize with our weaknesses, but we have one who has been tempted in every way, just as we are—yet he did not sin" (Hebrews 4:15). The Greek word for *empathize* that is used in this verse is the word *sumpatheó*; it means "to have a fellow feeling with, i.e., sympathize with."[2]

Jesus is able to empathize and sympathize with every feeling you've ever had. Pause. Think about that for a moment. Let that thought sink down deep into the crevices of your soul. How does that make you feel? Doesn't that make you feel heard, understood, and valued? Jesus understands every feeling you've ever experienced. When you pour out your heart to Him, He listens and empathizes. Isn't that incredible? He now invites you to follow His example and offer that empathy to others.

We are to learn to "carry each other's burdens," and in this way become more like Christ (Galatians 6:2–3). A large part of learning to help carry another's burden is offering empathy. You're probably thinking, *Great, Becky. But how? What does it look like to offer empathy?*

A great place to start is to learn how to validate another's feelings.

What Does It Mean to Validate Another's Feelings?

When you validate another person's feelings, you're basically saying, "Your feelings make sense." You compassionately acknowledge that the person's feelings are important and that those feelings are understandable. You don't correct feelings or instruct a person on how to feel. You simply offer understanding.

Two of Julie's kids were fighting. Words were flying and volume was rising. Finally, her son Zane lost it. Tempted to rebuke him, Julie paused and asked Zane to sit on the steps for a moment. Then she went and asked him to tell her what happened. Rather than starting with a rebuke and a lecture about controlling his emotions, Julie put the effort into understanding. She began by saying, "Wow, that must feel so frustrating to you. I understand why you felt so angry. Maybe next time you could . . ." The results were phenomenal. Instantly, Julie built a bridge to her son's heart by understanding his feelings.

The goal is to build bridges of connection by demonstrating that you care and value the relationship enough to validate what the other person is feeling. Now, in case that sounds hard, let me encourage you.

As women, we have the advantage here. Generally speaking, we're good at validating and empathizing. In fact, a study of 15,000 women by *Family Circle* found that women would rather talk to their girl-friends when they're feeling sad than to their spouses.[3] Why? Because we want to feel felt! Women for the most part are naturally better at sympathetic responses such as, "mm-hmmm" and "Go on."[4]

Your husband might be a rock star at empathizing, but apparently many are not. Don't give your hubby a bad time about this because it just might be the way his brain is wired. I remember when Steve and I were first married and Steve was completely baffled by my tears. I quickly learned that I needed a few good girlfriends who were good at empathizing and understanding tears. That didn't diminish my marriage. It made my marriage stronger.

Validate Feelings, Not Necessarily Actions

Validating someone's feelings doesn't necessarily mean you agree with the actions of the other person. It's extremely important to draw a distinction between *feelings* and *actions*. Feelings are neither right nor wrong. They're just feelings. It's what we do with those feelings that determines whether or not we sin. For example, suppose you feel hurt and angry because someone criticized you. The feeling of anger isn't wrong. This is why Paul wrote, "Be angry and do not sin" (Ephesians 4:26 ESV). If, however, you take action by rehearsing that anger over in your mind and you begin to talk badly about that person in your mind, your anger turns into bitterness. Bitterness isn't a feeling. It's a choice. And it's wrong. Jesus, though He understands our feelings and validates them, *never* validates sin. In our validating, we need to follow the example of Jesus.

Suppose your teen is at a party and a keg of beer is brought out. Other teens begin drinking even though they are underage. Your teen feels pressure—that's a feeling you can validate. It makes perfect sense why your teen would feel a lot of pressure in that circumstance. But what action they take as a result of the pressure will determine whether or not you can validate their actions.

This exact situation happened to one of my daughters when she was seventeen years old. She was at a party when all of a sudden a group of guys arrived with a keg of beer. When Keri saw the keg, she felt pressure, so she grabbed her car keys and left the party. The next morning when she told me what happened, I said, "Wow! You must have felt so much pressure. But you didn't cave. I'm so proud of you!" In that instance I was able to validate both the feeling and the action. But trust me, that wasn't always the case in our parenting journey.

The bottom line is this:

**Validate feelings,
but only validate actions that line up with Scripture.**

When You Can't Validate Actions

Sometimes we find ourselves tested in this principle, especially if we're people pleasers. Let's look at some typical scenarios where this principle might become difficult.

Listening to a Friend Complain About Her Marriage

Often when girlfriends get together, one of them will start criticizing their husband. In an effort to validate, it's easy to get sucked into enabling "husband bashing." This was the case for Tory.

Tory was having lunch with her friend Shelly. As the two women sat at an outdoor café, Shelly began to tell Tory about the current problems she was facing in her marriage. Shelly shot accusations against her husband out of her mouth faster than Tory could keep up with them. Tory felt so sorry for her friend! Her compassionate heart went out to her friend. As the two ate lunch, they cried together about the fact that Shelly's husband was being a jerk!

Later, Tory was reflecting back and praying for her friend. Sure, in many ways Shelly's husband was wrong. But with further thought and prayer, Tory realized that Shelly was contributing to the problem by enabling her husband's addictions. As Tory thought and prayed, she realized she could have validated feelings while still directing Shelly toward truth. After this enlightening thought, the next time one of Tory's friends shared a marital problem, the conversation went very differently.

When Leslie opened up about her marriage problems, Tory listened empathetically. She validated that the situation was rough, but then she posed the question, "Leslie, that must feel discouraging, but what are you doing to encourage your husband? Are you praying for him? Is there anything you could do differently?" Her sensitive questions prompted some introspection on Leslie's part, and the results were phenomenal. Leslie decided to put more effort into her marriage. She began praying faithfully for her husband and speaking affirmations to him daily. Tory and Leslie's friendship is still strong, but Tory didn't stoop to join in husband bashing. Instead, she validated feelings and then gently challenged her friend to value her husband by praying for him and encouraging him.

Listening to Gossip

Listening to gossip is wrong. Relational wisdom from Proverbs teaches us that just as gossip is wrong, so is listening to gossip: "Whoever utters slander is a fool" (Proverbs 10:18 ESV). "A gossip betrays a confidence, so avoid anyone who talks too much" (Proverbs 20:19). While most of the time we need to be concerned with validating, when gossip is involved, we need to be concerned that we *don't* validate. But this is easier said than done.

A group of friends gathers at Starbucks and, in between sipping lattes, the conversation turns to a mutual acquaintance. What begins as genuine concern quickly takes a turn for the worst and becomes gossip. What do you do? Do you listen and validate the "concern" expressed? Do you quickly turn the conversation toward prayer and suggest that everyone bow their heads at Starbucks and start praying? Do you sit quietly and ignore what's happening, hoping the conversation will end? Or do you blow the whistle and call your friends out on gossiping? How do you know when something is a concern and when it is gossip?

The tipping point is when the conversation becomes dishonoring of another. My daughter Keri was at a navy-wives gathering. One of the navy wives reached out to Keri and said, "Hey, have you met, Daphene? She's kind of weird, huh?" Keri takes honoring others very seriously, and immediately her radar went up, realizing the conversation was going in a bad direction. But Keri also doesn't enjoy confrontation, so she paused briefly and then replied, "Yes, I did meet Daphene, and I really liked her." Immediately, the conversation shifted. Without saying so, Keri sent the clear message that she wasn't going to enter into gossip.

You don't have to shame the person who is gossiping. You can use a soft tone and change the subject or say something honoring about the person who is the victim of the gossip. If the person gossiping is a close friend and gossiping seems to be a repeated pattern, you can gently say, "Hey, I'm uncomfortable with talking about someone behind her back. Let's hold each other accountable to only say what's honoring about others, okay?"

Girlfriends are invaluable. We empathize with each other and feel with each other, but in our caring, let's also gently encourage each other to mirror Jesus' listening style more effectively. One trait we can emulate is Jesus' compassion, especially when others are hurting. That is the exact time when it is essential that we carry each other's burdens. All of us will walk through seasons of pain. During those seasons, an empathetic listening ear can go a long way. Let's take a look at a few of those sensitive scenarios.

Sensitive Scenarios

Walking With a Friend through Grief

In every life there will be seasons of grief. As friends and lovers, we have the extraordinary privilege of walking alongside and offering empathy to one who is grieving. I love the example Jesus set by empathizing when Lazarus died. Jesus cried with Martha and Mary. No sermon. No pious platitudes. Simply listening and crying (John 11:36)!

I met Jacey at an event where I was speaking. During the course of our conversation she mentioned how she had suffered two miscarriages, both during her second trimester. My heart immediately went out to her because several who are close to me have also experienced that. I hugged her and listened as she shared some of her feelings, and then I asked her if she was receiving good support. She told me that while she was receiving good support now, the journey had been rough. Several well-meaning friends had made comments like, "Well, at least you still have two kids!" Even though Jacey does have two children, that truth doesn't take away from the pain of losing two others! Jacey was gracious in her response and understands that people are trying as best they can to comfort, but she also shared how painful those comments were to her fragile heart.

When author Dee Brestin lost her husband, Steve, to cancer, well-meaning people tried to enter her pain. But some friends tried to encourage by offering a sermon. Dee writes,

> Even condolence cards can twist the knife by giving you a little sermonette. When my husband was dying and suffering incredibly, I'd open up a card that said, "*All things work together for the good of those who love God and are called according to His purpose. (See Romans 8:28)."* And I'd want to scream, "How insensitive!" I know the above verse is true, but there is a time to speak it, and a time to be silent. High-tide grief calls for empathy, *not* solutions![5]

Kathy went through a horror that no parent ever wants to walk through. Her precious fifteen-year-old daughter, Leisha, was struck by a car while out jogging one afternoon and died instantly. I asked Kathy to talk about her journey with grief and describe what was helpful and what was not. Here's what Kathy wrote:

> It was not helpful when:

> - People insinuated how to grieve.
> - People gave trite answers to my pain.
> - People were afraid to let me talk about Leisha.
> - People tried to pretend it was going to be okay.

> The friends who were most helpful were just present in my life; they let me talk or be quiet, weep or laugh, fight or be still. They weren't afraid to enter into the silence or the wrestling. They weren't afraid to use Leisha's name or to hear yet another story about her. These people were true gifts to my soul.

Natalie echoed Kathy's words when I asked her about the grieving process after her husband, Drew, died. Natalie lost her husband unexpectedly while she was pregnant with their second son. Here are Natalie's words:

When Drew first died, people with great intentions poured out truths to me. "You will see him again!" "He is with Jesus!" And yes, these truths were paramount to my faith and hope, but the moments that most stand out, eight years later, are the moments that I was simply able to sit and grieve with someone. They sat with me in my grief. That sounds too simple, but often I think believers are uncomfortable with grief!

Yes, as believers we grieve as those who have hope, but often, I just needed someone to sit with me in my grief and in my wrestling with the Lord. I remember the day of Drew's memorial. I was exhausted afterward. I had had a very difficult time sleeping in the days after his death, and it had caught up to me and my pregnant belly. I fell asleep at my parents' house that afternoon, and when I woke up, my best friend was just sitting nearby me. She wasn't expecting me to talk or process through anything but she wanted me to know she was there for me, in my grief.

The presence of a friend who is willing to sit with someone in their grief, not with their own agenda but able to rest in grief with someone, is a powerful thing!

When your friends or loved ones are walking through the valley of grief, God will use you as you offer your listening presence, heartfelt tears, and practical acts of service. There's no need for sermonettes. Knowing you understand and feel with them is enough.

Helping a Child or Teen Deal with Anger or Frustration

Often in Christian circles there's confusion about anger. According to the Bible, anger is not wrong. It's a feeling (Ephesians 4:26). Rebuking kids for feeling angry doesn't accomplish anything except more frustration. Our focus needs to be on helping them deal with anger in an empathetic and productive way. When kids feel understood, they're more likely to receive our input on how to process their anger. It's wise to acknowledge and validate their anger, and then, when you're sure they feel understood, show them what it looks like to offer understanding and forgiveness.

Young children need a way to release those angry feelings because their feelings frighten them. A two-year-old throwing a fit needs to be held tightly and reassured of your love. A young child might need to stomp her feet, do an "angry dance," or draw a picture. When we empathize with kids' angry feelings, we assure them of our love and connection.

When our two youngest daughters were teens, Steve was being verbally attacked by critics in our church. Beyond the normal critical emails and notes, his antagonists were spreading nasty rumors, sending hate mail to the house, and petitioning for his resignation. My girls were ticked, and rightly so. Honestly, Steve and I felt concerned that because of the ugliness they were seeing at church, they would walk away from their faith.

One night when my brother-in-law, Craig, was visiting, he built a fire in the backyard and invited our teens to write angry messages to the people involved. Craig told my teen girls they could write whatever they wanted and that he wouldn't judge them for their feelings. He then invited them to toss those notes into the fire. It was a powerful exercise for my two teens and gave them a tangible method to release their anger. That little exercise around a fire pit ended up being a significant step toward our girls' letting go of their anger and ultimately offering forgiveness.

However you encourage your kids to release their anger, I caution you, don't rebuke or shame them for feeling angry. You want to build bridges to their hearts so that they continue sharing their feelings with you. Validate their feelings and help them process how they plan to release their anger.

Listening to a Loved One Who Is Depressed

Some Christians seem to get especially twisted in their thinking over depression. But depression is a complicated medical condition that often requires medical expertise. In order to be an empathetic, listening friend to a person struggling with depression, you need to understand that the brain is like a muscle. If you sprain a muscle in your ankle, you need ankle support, right? Similarly, if a brain is exhausted from excessive stress or trauma, a brain needs support. Sometimes that support needs to be in the form of medicine.

Unfortunately, many well-meaning listeners offer advice when someone is depressed, and sometimes the advice can be dangerous. For example, I have heard some give the advice that a person should "just" get off their antidepressant medicine. Unless you're a doctor, don't advise people to get off their meds. Instead, offer an empathetic, listening ear and model genuine faith.

Here are some practical ways to do this:

Offer to go for a walk with the person who is battling depression. As you walk and listen, two things happen. Walking releases endorphins and the person may begin feeling better, while listening will help them process their pain.

Ask gentle questions to help them shift their focus to God. Here are a few to get you started: "Where do you think God is in your pain?" "How do you best feel His presence?" If they say music, then you might suggest worship music to help heal the pain they're feeling. Ask if there's anything you can do for them. Running errands is a great practical method for encouraging the heart of someone who is battling depression, as depression zaps energy.

Listen attentively for clues. If you hear any sign of suicidal thoughts, take it seriously, and take action to keep the person safe. One way to do this is to ask questions to see if the person actually has a plan. Never agree to keep suicidal thoughts confidential, and don't validate suicidal thoughts. Instead, offer understanding, perhaps like this: "I can tell you feel hopeless right now. What would make you feel hopeful in this situation? I'm going to ask God to give you specific hope in your journey. Would you like to join me in asking Him to give you hope?" There are no easy answers for severe depression. Therapy and medical intervention might be necessary.

Sometimes, though, a person with depression simply needs to know that an empathetic person is cheering for them. Be the person who offers that gift.

The Gift of Empathy

The gift of empathy can change the entire nature of a person's life! Once a person feels understood, valued, and connected, they have hope and far less hostility. They are more willing to collaborate and solve problems. They are more able to learn, grow, and create. In essence, when a person feels understood, he or she is able to thrive and become the person God created him or her to be. As if that's not good enough, by offering empathy, you build the foundation for when conflict arises. The bottom line is that when people feel understood, they don't explode as easily. We'll be talking more about conflict in chapter 8, but for now, pause. Imagine for a moment how different your family would look if family members offered understanding. Imagine how different your church might look if people consistently reached out to others with empathy. Imagine how different your company might look if people listened empathetically to each other. Dream big. Imagine. What a different world we would live in if people consistently offered empathy.

EXERCISES TO
Strengthen Your Ear

Listening to God

1. Read Hebrews 4:15. What does this verse teach about the way Jesus empathizes with us? In what ways have you tangibly experienced Christ's empathy?

2. Read Psalm 23:4. The word for comfort used here means "to sigh with one who is grieving."[6] In what ways have you personally felt comforted by God?

3. Read the following verses. Each one contains the phrase "one another." Write one sentence next to each one describing the main point of the verse. Then spend a few moments reflecting on what God is speaking to you personally about empathy and "one another" living. Write down your thoughts.

   • Romans 12:10
   • Galatians 6:2
   • Ephesians 4:31–32
   • 1 Peter 3:8

Listening to Your Heart

4. Think back to a season when you were grieving. What did grief feel like to you? What felt most comforting to you during that season?

5. Think about a time when a friend was grieving. Did you offer any statement that felt like a trite platitude? What might you do differently next time?

Listening to Others

Plan a coffee date with a friend.

- On the way, plan specific questions to ask your friend about a stressful situation in her life. As you drive to meet her, ask God to help you to listen empathetically.
- As your friend processes her stress, refrain from any statement that might be perceived as "fixing." Focus instead on putting yourself in your friend's shoes. Offer understanding by validating the stress she is feeling. You might offer statements like, "That sounds very stressful," or "That must feel overwhelming."
- Ask specifically, "What can I do to support you?"
- Later, after you've left your friend, reflect on the time. What did you notice about yourself during this exercise? What did you learn about your friend? What did you learn about empathy? Write down your thoughts.

7

Watch Your Nonverbals— They're Speaking Loudly

If you're excited, tell your face about it. Your body language should match your words.

—Tony J. Hughes

Steve and I were reflecting openly and honestly about our marriage. We were both more relaxed than usual, so I ventured to ask a rather vulnerable question: "Babe, is there any part of our marriage that disappoints you?"

Steve stiffened slightly, signaling to me that he was nervous about where this conversation might be going. I remained quiet and still. After a long pause, he replied, "Hiking."

I was determined to keep the conversation safe for Steve to truly share his feelings, and that meant I couldn't sigh, roll my eyes, or knit my brow. I had opened a vulnerable conversation, and I needed to take responsibility to keep it safe. My nonverbal communication needed to be as inviting as the words I was speaking.

We had talked about hiking before, and Steve had expressed his desire for me to go more. I like hiking a lot. But Steve *loves* hiking. He would go for a hike every day if his schedule allowed. In the past, when hiking has come up, I've grown defensive and tried to prove how often I've gone hiking with him and why I can't go more often. But I wanted my husband to feel heard and honored, so I worked to stay relaxed now, not make any faces that would discourage conversation, and simply stayed present and interested.

The next morning, as I had some time with God, I wrote in my journal, *"Lord, please show me how to help Steve feel loved in the hiking department. Show me what I need to do. I want him to feel heard, loved, and treasured. I'm at a loss to know what to do because I've told him how much I enjoy hiking with him, but I feel like that's not what he's hearing."*

Later that day, Steve and I were browsing through an adventure store together that had hiking boots on sale. I randomly asked the store manager if I could try a pair on. Steve, who normally hates shopping and spending money, was absolutely thrilled that I was trying on hiking boots. We were having fun together. I knew we weren't there to buy anything, but I mentioned to him, "I wonder if I would feel more secure on some of the trails we hike if I had better ankle support?"

To my utter shock, Steve told me to pick out any pair I wanted and he bought them for me, even though they were very expensive.

That night, after reflecting on the day, I realized hiking boots were the answer to my prayers. My actions in trying on hiking boots and wanting a pair spoke louder than my words to Steve. And ironically, Steve's actions in spending the money on the hiking boots spoke louder than his words in showing me just how important hiking was to him.

The truth is, our actions always speak louder than our words. This is why we need to give attention to our nonverbal communication if we want to strengthen our relationships.

Nonverbal Communication

Nonverbal communication makes up between 60 and 75 percent of the impact of a message.[1] That's rather staggering when you think about it. You can choose your words carefully but blow the entire conversation if you're not careful with your body language and consistent with your actions.

Relational wisdom from Proverbs teaches that "fools show their annoyance at once" (Proverbs 12:6). How do you show your annoyance? You might roll your eyes, sigh, open your mouth in shock, frown, or cross your arms. All of those nonverbal expressions send a signal.

Our worlds are full of nonverbal signals that go beyond just what we do with our faces. "Non-verbal communications include facial expressions, the tone and pitch of the voice, gestures displayed through body language and the physical distance between the communicators."[2]

I recently heard that nearly every athlete who crosses a finish line throws his arms up in the air as a sign of victory. Even those blind from birth throw their arms up victory, though they've never seen another person do it. It's instinctual. Much of our nonverbal communication is instinctual, and that's exactly why we need to put in some effort. Without intentionality, what you've done for years will stay the same.

The signals you send during a conversation are vitally important to creating trust and transparency in your relationships. One article I read said:

> It's well known that good communication is the foundation of any successful relationship, be it personal or professional. It's important to recognize, though, that it's our nonverbal communication—our facial expressions, gestures, eye contact, posture, and tone of voice—that speak the loudest.[3]

Wow! When I first read that statement it startled me. I realized how important the signals I send to others are to establishing a close relationship built on trust and mutual respect.

Jesus used nonverbal communication perfectly. He cried at Lazarus's tomb (John 11:36). He held children on His lap and hugged them affectionately (Mark 10:13–16). I imagine Him waving to Zaccheus, asking him to come down out of the tree so that they could have dinner together (Luke 19:1–10).

My favorite story of Jesus' body language is when a rich man approached Jesus and asked, "What must I do to inherit eternal life?" (Mark 10:17). Jesus reminded the yuppie of the commandments. The young man assured Jesus he had kept them in perfect obedience. In response, Jesus paused and He "looked at him and loved him" (Mark 10:21). I love those words. Jesus was about to ask this young rising star to sell all his possessions, give everything to the poor, and come follow Him. Not a popular invite by anyone's standards. But first, He simply looked deeply into his eyes and loved him. Can't you just imagine the love Jesus' eyes held? Pause for a moment. That's the look His eyes hold for you.

In your relationships, what does it look like for you to mimic Jesus and show others how valuable they are? How does your face send the signal, "I want to hear what you have to say"? Your nonverbal signals act as a green light, inviting others to share their feelings, or as a red light, discouraging others from sharing their feelings. The bottom line is that if you want others to feel safe enough to let you see in their hearts, you've got to be mindful of the signals you're sending and put some effort into making sure those signals are inviting.

Let's get practical and think about some specific signals that are inviting, and figure out how we can implement them immediately.

Inviting Signals

Leaning

While You Were Sleeping is one of my favorite movies. Lucy is a lonely Chicago Transit Authority token collector until she saves Peter's life and his family mistakenly believes she is his fiancée. As the family waits for Peter to awaken from a coma, Peter's brother Jack begins to fall in love with Lucy. At one point in the story, Jack accuses Lucy of flirting with another man because she was "leaning." Lucy asks what he means, and Jack says, "Leaning is a lot different than hugging. Hugging, that involves arms and hands, and leaning is whole bodies moving in like this. Leaning involves wanting and accepting." Someone walks by and asks Lucy if Jack is bothering her. Lucy says no, and he replies, "Are you sure? 'Cause it looks like he's leaning."[4]

While the line about leaning describes romance, it also applies to general listening. One of the most inviting signals you can send to someone to invite them to talk is leaning toward the conversation. Leaning involves wanting and accepting. When we lean toward the person, we are sending the signal that we want to hear their words and receive them.

Our friend Greg is a great listener. When you're in a conversation with Greg, he leans toward you and you get the feeling he is hanging on your every word. As a result, you automatically become more willing to share what's on your heart. I've tried to adopt this practice when I'm out with friends.

Smiling

Another inviting signal to keep others talking is a warm, inviting smile. Michael Hyatt, former CEO of Thomas Nelson and author of the *New York Times* bestseller *Platform*, wrote a blog post that impacted me greatly. It was all about the power of smiling. In his post he told about a time when another employee thought he was mad because he wasn't smiling enough. In addition, his booking agent confronted him on smiling more when Michael was speaking. As Michael began to work on smiling more, he noticed that people were more drawn to him and that people felt much safer to communicate with him.[5]

Carol is a great example of this. I met Carol when I spoke at her church on Whidbey Island. I was instantly drawn to her because of her inviting smile. She sparkles! Every time I got up to speak, Carol had a huge smile on her face. Every time I saw her through the weekend, she was smiling, whether she was sitting at meals, chatting with friends, or taking notes during the conference. I've since learned about Carol that people in the grocery store often stop her to randomly ask her questions about which fruit is the best or what recipes she uses. No wonder! I think the reason Carol is so approachable is because she smiles all the time.

One year around the holidays, I got stuck in an airport for five unexpected hours. I decided to observe people and do a little experiment. Many travelers around the holidays are stressed. They walk through airports with slight frowns on their faces and look a bit intense. During part of my five-hour layover I decided to walk through the airport and simply smile at people. The response was amazing! Granted, some looked at me as though I were high on drugs, but most caught themselves and smiled back. Some even stopped to chat and tell me about their holiday plans.

I feel this is especially important with children. When our grandkids come over to our house, I try to show the excitement I feel to see them. When they see the sparkle in my eye and a big smile on my face, I am helping to build the "joy center" in their brains. "Joy is produced when someone is 'glad to see me.'"[6]

Try intentionally smiling wherever you are. Watch how people respond. My guess is they'll feel more drawn to you. And, as a bonus, smiling will actually elevate your mood.

Eye Contact

Maintaining eye contact is one of the most powerful ways to encourage another person to keep talking. A person's eyes tell you exactly where their focus is. Have you ever been starting to tell someone a story and noticed after you're only two seconds in that the person is looking at something else? Usually when a person breaks eye contact, they are sending the signal that the conversation is over. If they look down a lot, they may be sending signals of insecurity or self-doubt. If they look over your shoulder, they might potentially be bored or distracted.

If you want others to feel valued, look at them and listen. Don't get into a creepy staring contest, but simply maintain good, positive eye contact.

Nodding

When a person is sharing something vulnerable and you want to validate what they're feeling, nodding your head will help them feel understood. Nodding your head can send the signal that you understand and you want them to continue processing their feelings.

Avoiding a Shocked Face

In addition to nodding your head, avoiding a look of shock on your face will not cut the conversation short. On the other hand, if you drop your jaw and look horrified, the person speaking will likely stop. This is particularly true when you have teenagers involved.

Suppose your teen comes home and starts telling you about the party he attended the night before. He tells you that some of his friends pulled out a marijuana joint. If your mouth drops and your face looks angry, you won't hear another word, trust me. If, however, you don't look shocked but your face invites him to tell you more, he might keep going and let you know what happened next. Which I'm guessing you want to know, right?

In all honesty, I can't tell you how many times I messed this up as a parent. My facial expressions are very readable; the minute I look shocked, my kids stop talking. I finally learned that the best way I could hear information was when I was driving and they were looking straight out the front windshield while I was looking at the road. During our drive times, I learned a whole lot more about the issues and pressures my kids were facing. Gradually I began to realize how impactful my facial expressions were, and I began to intentionally work on sending more inviting signals to my kids.

A Bounce in Your Step

Even walking with a bounce in your step speaks a positive message.[7] Those who walk with a bounce are perceived as positive, and people are more drawn to them. Conversely, those who walk sluggishly with their heads down are often perceived as depressed or even crabby. And who wants to share their heart with someone crabby? Honestly, I think as women who follow Jesus, we need to be especially careful here. Many have the perception that Christians are cranky. I don't believe Jesus was cranky, do you? Let's put some effort into changing that perception by putting a little bounce in our step. We'll be far more pleasant and approachable, and more successful as well.

John Maxwell writes that an audience will draw conclusions about a speaker within the first seven seconds. He goes on to say that those who walk briskly and with a bounce in their step when approaching the platform will communicate their excitement to speak.[8] Who wants to listen to a speaker who's not even excited about their message or happy to be there?

Do yourself a favor—put a bounce in your step! Show others you're excited to see them and be with them. It will go a long way in building trust in your relationship.

Beyond sending inviting signals, you'll want to become an expert at reading other people's signals. Why? Because learning to read another person's signals correctly can make or break the relationship.

Learning to Read the Signals of Others

Think about a time when you met someone new for the very first time. Maybe you met at a church event, a networking event, or even on a date. Did they walk in confidently with a little bounce in their step? Were they smiling? Did they stand tall or slumped? Did they look you in the eye or peer nervously down at the floor? What conclusions did you draw after meeting them?

Think about the people closest to you. Maybe your spouse. How did he walk in the door after work yesterday? Was there a bounce in his step or did he drag his feet? Was he smiling or did he appear to be frowning? How was his tone as he discussed his day?

What about your co-worker? Was he frowning with a furrowed brow, looking tense, or sighing heavily at his desk? Did he walk out of the office with shoulders hunched, or did he walk confidently? All of those can be indicators of what type of day the people closest to you had. If you're going to build trust and transparency in your relationship, you need to learn to recognize those signals.

Several years ago, there was a show on television where the main character would figure out if the person was lying or not. While the show was a form of entertainment and not based on truth, there are universal body-language signs that someone will often use when lying. When a person is lying, eyes maintain little contact and tend to shift, perspiration increases, breathing rate increases, often the person has their hands in front of their mouth, complexion might change, and voice pitch might also change. Isn't that amazing? Those of you who are parents can learn to become skilled at observing those signals and you'll be able to figure out much more quickly when your kids are lying!

Learning to accurately assess body-language clues can also help you in the workplace. Can you read the signals of those working alongside you? Do you need a tip? Here you go.

I read this recently: "The normal blink rate is six to eight times a minute. But under stress, you'll blink more often and somewhat more dramatically."[9] Next time you're in a stressful meeting at work, if you want to know who's stressed out and who's cool as a cucumber, observe how many times someone is blinking! Beyond blinking, there are other clues to look for.

When you walk into a team meeting, pause for just a second and observe the body language of your fellow teammates. Do people have their heads down? Are some frantically checking email? Anyone seem relaxed and smiling? All of those can be indicators of what might need to happen in your meeting in order for it to be successful. During the meeting, keep your mind alert to how others are responding by observing what's happening with their bodies.

Teresa is a very successful leadership coach who is often brought in to companies to coach teams having difficulty moving forward with their goals. Teresa wrote to me about one situation where it became apparent very quickly what was slowing the team down. Here are Teresa's words:

> I stepped into the boardroom, meeting already underway, and quietly found my place along the wall. I watched as a somewhat heated discussion was in full force. There was a man leaning across the table, partially lifted from his seat. His index finger was pounding on the table in rhythm with his words. His voice was slightly raised and his eyes were fixed on the person across the table. All others in the room seemed to fade away in the midst of the conflict. His opponent was leaning forward, shaking his head with lips tight and thinned across his face and a squint in his eye. Frustration filled the boardroom as others gathered their things, whispering, "I'm outta here."
>
> About an hour later, I saw the two individuals who had gone head to head in the meeting sitting together at lunch and sharing some laughs. Intrigued, I sat down to talk to them. What these two had long forgotten was what their body language was saying to their entire organization. While they enjoyed the heated debates, they didn't understand the wall they were building. They had lost sight of the intended outcome—to have everyone's opinion count and to arrive at the best solutions for the success of the organization.
>
> I asked these two sparring opponents to try a few things: (1) to show up to the next project meeting and keep their backs pressed into their chairs, (2) avoid touching the table at all, (3) sit at the farthest distance from each other, (4) direct all of their questions to different people in the room to elicit input, and (5) speak in a slower and lower tone of voice.
>
> The meeting was amazing. The team was leaning in, excitedly adding their ideas and input. They stayed until the end of the

meeting and their energy was through the roof. What happened? We removed the negative body language and raised the self-awareness of those leaders. No matter how many words you use, your body language is speaking louder and stronger.

What Teresa described is often the norm not only in companies but also in churches and other nonprofits. If you want to understand those you live with, work with, worship with, and play with, practice your observation skills.

Intentionally Practice Your Observation Skills

Learning to enhance your observation skills is not as hard as you might think. The other day I decided to do this by watching the afternoon news without the sound on. I simply sat and observed the people being interviewed on the show. Even though the sound was turned off, I could tell immediately who was tense with whom and who held opposing points of view just by the way they were interacting with each other. Try it after you read this chapter. You'll be amazed by what you learn. Then take what you learned into your next conversation.

The next time you have lunch with a friend, co-worker, or spouse, reflect back afterward and ask yourself one or more of the following questions:

How was my eye contact, and how was theirs?

Did you both maintain eye contact or did one of you become distracted? Now, let me warn you, the purpose of asking yourself this is to monitor your body language and become attentive to theirs. It is not for you to observe and then criticize your husband because he didn't maintain eye contact! This is for observation purposes only. Absolutely do not—and I repeat, DO NOT—allow yourself even a second of judging.

What did I learn from the person's facial expression?

Did they smile? Have a furrowed brow? Did they look tense or frustrated? Did their eyes look tired? If they did look tired, please don't say, "You look tired today!" That comment always makes people feel like they need more concealer under their eyes. Simply observe so you can empathize with whatever is shared in the conversation.

What did their use of personal space show me?

Some people close to you are huggers and some are not. When you were in conversation with your friend, did you give them a warm hug? Did you maintain personal space, or did you stand too close? How did they respect your personal space? Would you describe your friend as a hugger? Why or why not? Learning the personal space cues of others is important to becoming people smart. So learn to observe how close a person likes to stand.

What did I learn from the other person's posture?

First, evaluate your posture. Did you lean toward them as they were speaking?

What did you learn from their posture? Were they slouching or sitting up straight and tall? I can often tell when someone has self-esteem issues based on their posture. Those who are confident will walk into a room with their heads held high; those carrying emotional loads of shame or insecurity will often walk into the room hesitantly, head down, and when they sit they often pull their arms in close as if protecting their body.

As you reflect back on your time, was your friend fidgety or did they seem calm and collected? How did you draw that conclusion?

How did I invite my friend to continue talking without using my words?

After you've asked these questions, spend some time reflecting. Did you lean toward your friend and nod as they chatted?

Show Them You Care

The apostle Paul gave great advice for showing others that you truly care about them. He wrote, "Rejoice with those who rejoice, weep with those who weep" (Romans 12:15 ESV). What's amazing about Paul's instructions to us is that much of it can be done without words. Think of how you might celebrate with others before you ever use your words. You could give them a high five or applause. You could have a twinkle in your eyes as you celebrate their accomplishments. And even if tears don't come when you are commiserating with others, they can usually tell by your eyes if you really feel their pain.

I want to send inviting signals to the people in my life so that they feel safe to share their hearts. I want my body language to express to them that I'm available and ready to listen. In the next chapter, we'll be talking about handling conflict. Your body language is critical when you're having a disagreement with someone. Before you begin the next chapter, why don't you take a moment and pray this prayer:

Lord Jesus, I long to be like you and look at others with eyes of love. I want my family, friends, colleagues, and neighbors to see your love in my eyes and feel your love for them through my body language. Keep me from putting up any walls that would prohibit others from seeing you and experiencing your love. Let them sense inviting signals from me so that they feel honored and valued.

Listening to God

1. Read Mark 10:21. Now go back and focus only on the first sentence, "Jesus looked at him and loved him." Substitute the pronoun *him* with the pronoun *me* so that the sentence reads, "Jesus looked at *me* and loved *me*." Read that out loud several times. Then close your eyes and say that sentence to yourself. Imagine Jesus looking deeply into your eyes with eyes of love. Journal about what His eyes look like and what you feel in response.

2. Read John 11:35–36. How do you think the Jews knew Jesus loved Lazarus? Think back on a situation in your life that was painful. Then spend a few moments imagining Jesus weeping with you about the pain you experienced. How would it impact you to know that Jesus actually wept with you because of the pain you felt?

3. Spend a few moments listening to "Beloved" by Leeland. What did God speak to you as you were listening?[10]

Listening to Your Heart

4. When you feel annoyed or impatient, how does that typically play out in your body language?

5. Think back on a recent conversation with someone close to you. Were your nonverbals inviting? Is there anything you could do differently next time?

6. Can you think of five benefits to smiling? You might listen to Michael Hyatt's podcast "The Secret Power of Smiling" to get your thoughts moving.[11]

Listening to Others

7. During your next conversation with someone close to you, practice leaning toward them, smiling if they have something positive going on, or mirroring their sadness if they express pain. Afterward, record your thoughts about the conversation.

8. When your family arrives home today, show them with your face, your tone, and the bounce in your step how excited you are to see them. If you live alone, practice these skills with a friend or neighbor.

8

Seek to Understand During Conflict

See conflict not as a problem to be managed or resolved
but as an opportunity to strengthen the common life.
—Michael Hyatt

A people-pleaser by birth, I hate conflict. Yet, like everyone else I know, arguments have been a part of my close relationships. Looking back, I haven't always handled those well. Occasionally, I ignored, ran away from, or hid from disagreements, trying to keep peace at any and all costs. Now and then I may have come on too strong, wanting to prove my point, hoping against all odds that I was right. Often, I became paralyzed during tense conversations and, not knowing what to say next, I silently built a wall to protect my heart.

I mistakenly thought a "good Christian girl" like me shouldn't have any conflict in her life. If the Gospel transformed me, wouldn't it make sense that people would like me more and get upset with me less? If I was living close to Jesus, wouldn't that automatically mean my opinions were right? Shouldn't we all get along—All. The. Time? Could anything good come from conflict? Those questions and others sent me on a journey to understand my own responses in conflict and to shift my focus to the transformation that could result from arguments.

The first step on my growth journey was figuring out what messages I had received in childhood about conflict. I needed to understand the *why* behind my responses before change was possible.

My childhood home was very authoritarian. Issues were considered black or white, with very little room for gray. Though there was tension and anger, most of it was swept under the carpet. Messages like, "Hurt feelings are wrong," "Don't cry," "Protect the image," and "Keep family secrets" all played a significant role in my desire to keep others happy. The sexual abuse I experienced as a child stole my innocence and my voice. It left me feeling ashamed, angry, powerless, and without a safe place to express those feelings. As a child, I coped by pretending. I simply imagined a perfect world where everyone was happy with me.

My Pollyanna view didn't hold up when I became an adult. Though I tried as hard as I could to keep the peace with everyone, I experienced tension in friendships, ministry, and even in my marriage.

Relationships are very important to me, and that meant I had to figure out how to leverage conflict to strengthen those relationships rather than allowing disputes to weaken them. In pursuit of truth, I asked God for the courage to take an honest look at my methods of handling disagreements, because those methods were no longer working for me. Jesus said, "You will know the truth, and the truth will set you free" (John 8:32).

One of the first truths I realized about myself was that when I felt threatened, my ability to listen shut down. It was as if an automatic switch in my head cautioned me to be on the defense. Before I could listen to understand when in an argument, I had to feel safe. If I panicked, I knew I would come on too strong to prove my point or back off entirely and acquiesce to whatever the demand. I needed to shift my thinking. When others felt upset with me, it wasn't the end of the world. It might just mean that they had a need that wasn't being met. Similarly, being wrong wasn't catastrophic, it only meant I needed to apologize.

Truths About Conflict

In my quest for growth, I learned three basic truths about conflict:

Conflict Is Inevitable

The first truth I accepted was that conflict in this life is inevitable. As long as we live in a fallen world, conflict is going to be a part of it. If you doubt that, watch the evening news. People are going to hold different opinions and become angry at times. Occasionally their anger will drive them to hurt another. This is even true in our closest relationships.

The sad truth is that people are going to get mad at me, and it's not going to feel good. Some are not going to like my decisions and they're going to criticize. Others are just plain not going to like me!

Unfortunately, the same holds true for you. Conflict in your life is inevitable. The people closest to you as well as those not so close to you are not going to agree with everything you choose. Whether it's with your spouse, your kids, your neighbors, your friends, or your co-workers, you're going to have disagreements, tense conversations, and arguments. Until you accept that truth, conflict is going to freak you out.

Conflict Is Uncomfortable

The second truth I accepted is that conflict is uncomfortable. I like warm, fuzzy feelings that accompany believing everyone is in love with me and thinks I'm wonderful. Don't you? When you're in a conflict, it's not going to feel warm and fuzzy. It's going to feel uncomfortable.

Relational wisdom from Proverbs suggests, "Better a dry crust with peace and quiet than a house full of feasting, with strife" (Proverbs 17:1). No kidding! Who wouldn't rather have a small dinner with peace and tranquility than a feast with a lot of fighting? Let's face it: people get cranky and out of sorts. Disputes and disagreements don't make us feel happy and peaceful. When our homes, churches, or workplaces are filled with contention, it's a bust. But if you accept the truth that conflict is going to feel uncomfortable, you'll be able to listen more effectively, and you might even discover that conflict can be transformational.

Conflict Can Be Transformational

The third and most powerful truth I discovered is that conflict can be transformational. In the chaos of an argument, if you will listen to understand and focus on meeting the other's need, you'll be more able to work as a team, coming up with a solution that satisfies both. In the end, your relationship will emerge stronger and more resilient.

Remember the discussion I had about hiking with Steve? By focusing on listening rather than defending, we were able to come out of that discussion with a shared goal: hiking experiences that satisfied us both. Steve understood I needed better support for my ankle. I understood he needed more excitement from me about going on hikes. I walked away with hiking boots. Steve walked away with more hikes. It was a win-win. In fact, two nights ago we went for a hike that was awesome.

The comfort in all this is that Jesus experienced lots of conflict. He understands and empathizes. Though He himself was perfect, He lived life in our very imperfect world, and friction seemed to follow Him. If we study His life, we'll walk away with principles that will help us to navigate disagreements in such a way that transformation is possible.

Jesus Was Well Acquainted With Conflict

Though Jesus experienced lots of conflict, He didn't panic. His hands didn't get sweaty and His breath didn't get short. He didn't run from skirmishes or hide from scuffles. He calmly handled disagreements and disputes. No matter who was ticked at Him, Jesus remained calm and confident. Let's take a look at some different scenes from Jesus' life and observe the way He handled conflict.

When Confronted by His Friends

Jesus didn't try to keep everyone happy. How freeing! Right? One time when Jesus' disciples couldn't find Him, they became indignant and confronted Him, saying, "Everyone is looking for you!" (Mark 1:36). Clearly, they felt annoyed that Jesus would indulge himself and take time alone when there were many waiting to be healed. Jesus calmly listened and offered grace. He didn't remind them that He was the Almighty One who really didn't need their earthly wisdom to run His schedule. He simply said, "Let's go somewhere else so I can preach there as well" (Mark 1:38, my paraphrase). Don't you love it? Even though He sensed tension in the air, He didn't get defensive or frazzled. He didn't overexplain or try to convince His friends that He had chosen what was most important. He simply said, "We're going to the next town." He valued His friends' opinions but didn't feel pressured by them.

When Religious Leaders Tried to Pull Him Into Arguments

He knew when to pause and when to press His point. When the religious leaders dragged the woman caught in adultery to Jesus, demanding that He stone her, Jesus said nothing for a few minutes. Not. A. Word. He simply wrote in the sand. Then He invited those without sin to throw the first stone (John 8:1–11).

When on Trial Before Pilate

When Pilate asked Jesus if He was the king of the Jews, Jesus asked Him what other people had said about Him. Knowing that Pilate might feel threatened, Jesus offered understanding and explained to Pilate that His kingdom was not of this world. When Pilate asked Jesus where He came from, He didn't answer. He wasn't interested in arguing the validity of His deity (John 18:28–38).

With Peter After the Resurrection

Peter had denied Christ the night that Jesus was betrayed. Jesus must have felt hurt by Peter's denial, but His relationship with Peter was important to Him. He purposely pursued reconciliation with Peter. Gently yet firmly, Jesus gave Peter three opportunities to state his love for Him (John 21:15–18). As a result, Peter's relationship with the Lord was strengthened and transformed. Church history tells us that Peter was ultimately willing to die for his faith.[1]

When I reflect on those stories, I realize there are some very practical principles that I can draw from Jesus and put into practice in my own life that will help me listen more effectively when I'm experiencing conflict.

Practical Principles for Listening in Conflict

Pause

Jesus knew when to pause and when to push. Similarly, when you feel tension in a relationship, pause and pray. Often, in conflict, our adrenaline speeds up and we talk faster. Instead, pause, pray, and praise God that you don't have to feel panic. Breathe. Don't say anything for a few minutes. Don't interrupt. Simply let the other person process and fill in with "mm-hmms" and empathetic "oh's." When you do talk, talk slower and softer than your normal pace and tone.

Recently, Steve was coaching a young pastor who was about to face a tense board meeting where he knew his ideas were going to be met with opposition. Steve coached, "Talk slow, low, and last without flinching!" Good recommendation for any leader. That's exactly what Jesus did when the religious leaders dragged the woman caught in adultery to Him and demanded that He stone her. Jesus paused. He allowed several minutes of silence. When He spoke, He spoke slow, low, and last without flinching!

I needed to remember this rule when we were raising our kids. Our daughter Stef loved to negotiate with us. Knowing that Stef was going to launch into a well-scripted argument, I would have my defenses up the minute I felt tension in the air. Once my defenses were up, I couldn't hear what Stef was asking or arguing for. When Stef was about five years old, she caught on to how I would shut down and developed a new strategy. She would begin by saying, "Mommy, don't say no yet!" It was such a great reminder to me to pause, pray, and let her finish before saying no.

One time after I returned from a speaking event and Stef started in on why she needed a TV in her room, I was too exhausted to even listen. I paused and prayed, and God gave me a fabulous idea. I told Stef to go up to the computer and write me a full proposal complete with good sentence structure, punctuation, and paragraph formation. Stef took my challenge and spent two hours writing her proposal, and honestly, it was so compelling we let her have a 21-inch black-and-white TV in her room that only worked on one channel. I think she only watched it twice, but she felt like we heard her heart.

The point is to pause, pray, and slow down in your response. You'll be amazed at how pausing and praying can help you navigate tense conversations more effectively.

Listen for Something to Agree With

When you're in a conflict, challenge yourself to search diligently for some point to agree with. My theory is that if you listen to find a point to agree with, you won't be as uptight in the conversation. It's amazing how the climate of a conflict changes when one person says they agree.

Imagine that you and a good friend are out to lunch. As you're munching on your Caesar salad, your friend announces her support for a candidate you strongly disagree with in the upcoming election. You're shocked and almost choke on the crouton in your mouth! None of your other friends support that candidate, and you thought you were all in the same camp. How do you respond? Do you correct your friend and launch into an argument supporting your choice of candidate? Do you roll your eyes and ask why on earth she is supporting the opposing candidate?

Instead of choking, I'd like to suggest that in a friendly, non-confrontational tone, you ask what she likes about her candidate. After she responds, find something—anything—to agree with. For example, maybe she loves her candidate's heart for the poor. Certainly, you can agree. Jesus also had a heart for the poor.

Here's another example. As I write this chapter, Steve and I are getting ready to buy a house. Steve loves the wilderness and wildlife. I love having neighbors close by. Steve loves lots of mature trees. I like fewer trees and big picture windows so I can see the sky. Steve likes pine trees. I like palm trees. By the way, there aren't any palm trees in Colorado, but you get the picture. We think differently.

Yesterday, Steve and I were driving through a neighborhood and saw a house that I loved. We stopped and went through the house, and I was smitten! Steve wasn't so sure. There were neighbors close and not many trees. But then we went to the backyard, which looked out over a wilderness of trees, shrubs, and a few pines. Immediately, Steve said, "Oh, this is awesome! I could do this, babe!" He found something to agree with. He could put up with no trees in the front yard as long as he had the backyard.

The bottom line is, whether in friendship, marriage, or with co-workers, find a point of agreement and you'll dial down the tension in an argument.

Stay Curious

What do I mean by this? Often in a heated discussion or argument we plan what we're going to say next to prove our point. Instead of planning what you're going to say next, listen attentively to what the other person is feeling in order to understand. Remember, Jesus offered understanding to Pilate, and explained that His kingdom wasn't of this world. You can't offer understanding if you're busy planning what you're going to say next. The apostle Paul reminds us not to only look to our own interests but also to the interests of others (Philippians 2:4). When you stay genuinely curious to understand the other person's point of view, you are displaying the same attitude as Jesus.

Let the Other Person Finish Dumping

What do I mean? When a person is venting, crying, yelling, or simply complaining, give them time to finish. Don't interrupt. Don't offer solutions. Don't defend yourself. Why? Because a person who dumps is emotional and will feel exhausted afterward. An exhausted brain can't receive any input.

I learned this the hard way. Our teenage daughter was hurt and mad at me. In addition, she was stressed over exams, AP history, and problems in youth group. I went her room to talk, and she started to dump. Her emotions were escalating, and I kept trying to fix things for her. My intentions were good. I loved my daughter more than she could understand, but I handled the situation completely wrong. Stef vented and I interrupted. Stef sobbed, "You're not listening!" How could she say that? I was clearly listening. I was hearing every word loud and clear. I was trying to fix it and solve it so that both of us would feel peaceful. The more I tried to fix, the more hysterical Stef became. Finally, praise God, Steve came into the room and took over. He simply let Stef dump. He held her and let her sob. He allowed her to release every feeling without judgment.

Talk about a mom fail! I was pretty sure this one was up there with the worst of the worst! Later that night Steve said, "Beck, when she's upset she can't receive anything you're saying. Just let her dump. She loves you and you love her. You just have to let her get her feelings out. You can work out a plan to solve things later, but not in that moment." Wow. Steve was so right.

The same principle applies whether with your mother, your siblings, your kids, your spouse, or your co-workers. People who are venting can't receive your input. Their brains simply can't handle it. So do yourself a favor and let them vent. In fact, go one step further. When the person is venting, ask them to tell you more. By inviting them to tell you more, you keep it safe for them to exhale all the toxic feelings. After those toxins are released, they'll feel better. Give it some time, and then when everyone's emotions have settled, work out a solution together.

Manage Your Self-Talk

The conversation that's happening out loud is only half the argument. Often the most important conversation is the one happening in your head. Have you ever noticed what happens in your head when you're in a conflict? You imagine scenarios that may not be true. Perhaps your friend calls and says she's had a rough day and she's canceling coffee. It's the third time she's canceled. In your mind you start spinning a story. She's tired of you. She doesn't value the friendship with you. She always makes excuses.

Instead of tripping down the "poor me" lane, manage your self-talk. Ask what happened during her day and empathize. Shift your focus from your unmet needs to her unmet needs.

Affirm How Much You Value the Relationship

If you can't reach a compromise, it's good to say something like, "We have our differences, but I want you to know I love you and I'm committed to our relationship." I love this suggestion about conflict from Michael Hyatt: "Envision a shared future."[2] You might consider how you can both walk away from this conflict with a deeper and more fulfilling relationship.

129

A Few Tips to Avoid Conflict in the First Place

We've looked at some practical tools to help you to listen when you're experiencing a conflict, but since none of us enjoy conflict, I want to give you a few tips to help you listen and avoid some conflicts in the first place.

Let Go of the Need to Be the "Fact Police"

There is nothing more annoying than telling a story and having someone interrupt you to correct some tiny detail of your story. Right? If you tend to be the fact police, let it go. For example, suppose your spouse is telling a story about your vacation last summer and he gets some detail wrong. If it doesn't affect the story, you don't need to correct him. Honestly, nothing destroys intimacy in marriage like one partner who feels their calling is to correct the other with every detail. The same principle holds true with your friends. Let your friends tell their stories. It's okay if they get a few details wrong. They don't need you to be the fact police. Jesus said, "Do not judge" (Matthew 7:1). When you monitor and edit someone else's storytelling, it's judging. Instead, let it go.

Ask for Clarification

The writer of Proverbs says, "The discerning heart seeks knowledge" (Proverbs 15:14). One of the best methods I know for gaining discernment is to ask for clarification when you're listening. Often by asking someone to clarify what they meant, you can avoid arguments.

My friend Poppy tells about a time when she was baking scones.

After baking some scones that came out of the oven hard, flat and pale brown, I asked Jim if he'd like one. Glancing at them he asked, "Are they stones?"

His question struck me as funny, as well as an accurate description of my culinary offering. Laughing at his comment, I agreed that they did look like stones. To my surprise, Jim said, "I didn't call them stones. I said scones. You misheard me."[3]

What could have led to hurt feelings served as a reminder to Poppy to ask for clarification, and it saved Poppy from unnecessary conflict. The same principle will work well for you. Do yourself a favor: Before you get all up in arms, ask for clarification, because the other person might mean something entirely different from what you are imagining.

Make It Your Practice to Make People Feel Important

I'm not sure I can prove this with scientific facts, but it's my theory that those who seek to make others feel valued and important experience less conflict than those who don't. It makes sense, doesn't it? When people feel valuable, they're less likely to attack.

Mary Kay Ash, the founder of Mary Kay Inc., wisely said, "Everyone has an invisible sign hanging from their neck saying, 'Make me feel important.'"[4] Mary Kay knew how important it was to make women feel important. As a result, her cosmetic company was wildly successful. When you choose to make others feel important, you help take away the angst that somehow they don't measure up. If you make it your practice to look for ways to show people how valuable they are, you'll enjoy happier, more fulfilling relationships.

Psychiatrist and author Mark Goulston writes that one thing most "high-maintenance, easy-to-upset, difficult-to-please people have in common is that they feel as if the world isn't treating them well enough."[5] When people don't feel valued, they try harder to prove their importance, shout their opinions, and overpower others. According to Mark, if you want those people to stop driving you crazy, the answer is to give them some of what they need. Make them feel important. I recently heard John Maxwell speak at a live training for coaches. He instructed us as coaches to put a ten on everyone's head. His theory is that most people wonder if they're good enough. By viewing them as tens, you send the message that they are valuable, and that's what most are looking for. In other words, treat other people with honor and respect. Give them the value they long for, and you'll likely experience less conflict.

There is one exception to that rule that I feel the need to share.

What About Toxic People?

Generally speaking, you want to take your relationships deeper. That's why we've been studying how to listen so that people will talk. We want others to feel deeply valued. There are times, though, when because of the extreme brokenness of our world, a person is toxic, and it becomes unsafe for you to deepen a relationship. In those cases you need to pray about putting distance in your relationship. Toxic people want to attack you and destroy your world. They are bullies or "me centered" people who want to blame you for all their problems, manipulate, and attack you at the same time. Jesus calls us to be kind to everyone, but He also commands us to flee from evil (1 Thessalonians 5:22).

I asked a couple of my friends who are licensed therapists about toxic people, and Jill Lillard gave me three questions that she encourages her clients to ask themselves when dealing with a seemingly toxic person:

1. Are they people who will continue to be in your life (perhaps co-workers or family members)?

2. Are they toxic in general, or are they like peanuts—they make *you* anaphylactic but may not bother others?

3. Why are they toxic? (Do they incite fear, drain your energy, or are abusive?) I think the *why* helps you determine what sort of boundaries are needed and allows you to do a "cost and benefit" analysis of the relationship.

Here's the deal: You need a plan to deal with toxic people.

The Pharisees tried to bully Jesus, and you may remember that Jesus had some tough words for the bullies. He told them they were making others twice as much sons of hell as they were (Matthew 23:15). Often when we think about Jesus we don't imagine Him speaking such a strong rebuke to people.

When a toxic person is attacking, I find it best to follow these three rules:

- Don't get pulled in.

- Dial down your emotion.

- Back up and limit your contact.

Recognize that the person attacking you has a mental issue. It's easy to feel fear in those situations, but fear will encourage them to continue abusing you. Instead, try to listen without showing any emotion, and then back up. If you don't engage, you take away the other person's power to hurt you.

Please note: If you are being physically abused, don't stay in the relationship. Leave and get help. At the end of this chapter, you will find an additional recommended reading list to help you deal with conflict and toxic people.

In the next chapter, we'll be talking about being present and giving another person your undivided attention while they're talking. But first, here's a prayer for you.

The Perfect Prayer for Conflict

As we conclude this chapter, I think the perfect prayer for listening during a conflict would be the one that St. Francis of Assisi prayed. You're probably familiar with it, but take a few minutes and really pray the prayer. Ask the Lord to form His attitude in you as you grow in your ability to listen in conflict.

Lord, make me an instrument of Your peace. Where there is hatred, let me sow love; where there is injury, pardon; where there is doubt, faith; where there is despair, hope; where there is darkness, light; where there is sadness, joy.

O, Divine Master, grant that I may not so much seek to be consoled as to console; to be understood as to understand; to be loved as to love; For it is in giving that we receive; it is in pardoning that we are pardoned; it is in dying that we are born again to eternal life.[6]

Additional Recommended Reading

Crucial Conversations: Tools for Talking When Stakes Are High by Kerry Patterson, Joseph Grenny, Ron McMillan, and Al Switzler

Necessary Endings by Henry Cloud

Boundaries by Henry Cloud and John Townsend

Stop Walking On Eggshells by Paul Mason and Randi Kreger

Bold Love by Dan Allender and Tremper Longman

Listening to God

1. Read Matthew 5:9. Jesus said, "Blessed are the peacemakers." The word that Jesus used for "peacemakers" implies reconciliation. It doesn't mean keep the peace at any and all costs. In your opinion, what is the difference between peacemakers and peacekeepers? What do you feel God is speaking to you about you being a peacemaker?

2. Scripture teaches us that we were once in conflict with God (Romans 3:23) and that God took the initiative to pursue reconciliation with us. Jesus came as the one who would bridge the gap in our conflict and provide peace for us with God the Father. Read Romans 5:1. What does this verse speak to you personally? According to this verse, how can you be sure you are at peace with God the Father?

3. As you reflect back on this chapter, what do you feel God is speaking to you about the good that can come out of conflict?

Listening to Your Heart

4. What are some of the messages you received about conflict from your childhood?

5. In what ways might God want to reshape your thinking about disagreements?

6. Think about the last conflict you had with someone close to you. Describe the conversation you had in your head during the conflict. What did you learn about how you react in conflict?

Listening to Others

7. Think back to a conflict you had with someone recently. How is your relationship stronger now as a result of that conflict?

8. What did you learn in this chapter about the importance of letting another "dump" without interference? How might that shape your response the next time you have a conflict with someone in your family?

9. Think of someone you have a relationship with who is difficult. What do you think is the need behind the behavior that you find difficult? Is there anything you can do to meet that need? If so, journal about an action plan.

10. What is one tangible takeaway from this chapter that you will implement the next time you find yourself in a conflict with another person?

9

Let Go of Distractions

Being heard is so close to being loved that for the average person *they are almost indistinguishable.*

—David Augsburger

Stefanie wanted to talk about her AP history course but realized quickly that her dad was checked out.

Stef tried one more time. "Dad, for my AP history course I want to write my paper on the AIDS crisis in Africa. Which country would you suggest?"

Steve mumbled, "Uh huh, that's great, sweetie."

The weeks before had been stressful for Steve, and his mind had been a whirlwind thinking about upcoming meetings, staff difficulties, and financial pressure. Clearly, he wasn't processing anything Stef was trying to communicate.

Finally, Stef said, "Dad, I'm just going to go out and milk the cow." Steve muttered, "Okay, sweetie." Stef died laughing, and so did the rest of us, because we lived in suburban California and certainly did not have a cow.

The kids still tease Steve about that discussion. But the truth is, I've been just as guilty of being distracted as Steve, particularly during stressful seasons. There have been times when someone's been talking to me and I've been "out to lunch" in my mind, planning the next chapter in an upcoming book, deciding what I'll cook for dinner that night, or thinking about a problem a family member is facing.

Let's face it, we've all been guilty.

Maybe you have

- glanced at your phone to check a text message while a friend has been pouring her heart out to you;
- redecorated your bedroom in your mind while your husband was telling you about an exciting new opportunity;
- checked your email while on the phone with your mom;
- updated your Facebook status while your son was trying to tell you about his math assignment.

We've certainly all noticed when someone has not been present to us.

Maybe you have

- tried to talk to your husband while he's been engrossed in a football game;
- told a story to your friend and realized she didn't hear a word because a message came in on her phone;
- attempted to propose a new idea to your boss and watched as he tuned you out to check his email.

Based on the truth that we've all been guilty of distraction and been the victim of distraction, let's establish the ground rule for this chapter. Fair? The ground rule will be one word: *grace*.

We all need it and we all need to offer it because life is full of stress, demands, stimulation, and distraction. Together, we're going to set a personal growth goal of being attentive to others. But as we move forward toward that goal, we're going to offer others grace, realizing that everyone is at a different point in their journey.

The bottom line is this: People are dying to feel heard, and unless we purpose in our hearts to offer our full presence to others, we'll drift through life distracted and dishonor those who matter to us in the process. The truth is, God wants you to honor others by letting go of whatever is distracting you while they're talking.

Honoring Means Being Present

As we talked about in chapter 3, honoring one another is mandated biblically. The apostle Paul wrote that we are to "honor one another above yourselves" (Romans 12:10). When we think of honor, we might think of those who have earned respect: leaders, parents, people who have served in the military, or those who have lived lives of integrity and significance. The word for *honor* that Paul uses here carries the idea of affirming intrinsic value. In other words, we are to value people because each person has been created in the image of God. When we honor one another, we esteem others and demonstrate that we care about them.

One of the most effective methods of honoring another is to offer your full presence to the person talking. Spiritual director Henri Nouwen said, "To care means first of all to be present to each other."[1] Present. Not checked out. Not distracted. Not planning next week's board meeting. When we're present, we're aware and attentive to the person we're with. We're fully engaged.

Relational wisdom from Proverbs echoes this truth: "Pay attention and gain understanding" (Proverbs 4:1). That simple instruction applies to your relationships. Whether at home, at work, at church, or at your community center, the principle is clear: The way to honor someone is to listen and offer your focused attention.

Do you realize how rare this is in our day and age? We're overcommitted, overcaffeinated, and overstimulated. We have a plethora of communication apps at our fingertips that offer continual distraction. Our overstimulated minds are losing their ability to focus on quiet conversation with one person. I've been as guilty as you, and that's why we both need to pray that God will help us to see people as individuals dying to be heard.

When we become followers of Jesus Christ and are filled with His Spirit, our lives are radically transformed. Changed. Part of the transformation that takes place is learning to value people as much as God does.

John Maxwell talks about learning the art of "walking through a room slowly." I love that! Whether I'm with family, close friends, or at a speaking event, I try to remember to walk slowly and take the time to stop and listen. Rather than concentrating on what's happening next, what I need to finish, where I need to go, or how I need to get there, I want to focus on those around me. My desire is to honor each one as a person of intrinsic value who deserves my full attention. I don't always do this well. I tend to be a bit spacey. I'm always thinking but not always focused. I've been known to try to get in the wrong car simply because it's the same color as mine. Other times, I've been so wrapped up in my thoughts that I pass by someone I know very well and don't realize it till afterward. Ugh. I'm asking God to help me let go of the issues that are distracting me from being a focused and attentive listener because I want to send the clear message, "You have worth and value. You're important to me."

Jesus illustrated this beautifully. Remember the woman at the well? Though she was a woman with a sketchy past and a sordid present, Jesus offered her His undivided attention.

Can I Have a Drink?

Jesus, tired from His journey, took a break and stayed behind to rest when His disciples went searching for lunch. As He was resting, a Samaritan woman came to draw water from the well (John 4:1–26).

Most women didn't draw water at noon. The usual practice for women at this time was to go to the well early in the morning before the heat of the day. It was a social event—much like meeting your girlfriends at Starbucks might be today. But this woman came alone. Likely the other women in town didn't want to be with her because she had such a questionable reputation.

I don't know about you, but it's hard for me to listen attentively when I'm tired and hungry. But Jesus, though He was also tired and hungry, and enjoying a few moments of alone time, took the initiative to open a conversation. He asked for a drink of water. As she drew water from the bottom of the well, Jesus drew out her story from the depths of her soul. He honored her by giving His undivided attention and eventually revealing His true identity. His attentiveness became transformational for the woman; Scripture tells us that she put her faith in Christ. When she left the well that day, her life was completely changed!

I'm intrigued with Jesus. When I'm tired I prefer to zone out, and when I'm famished I can get "hangry"! Even though I'm an extrovert by nature, every now and then I simply need a break. I might turn off my phone, take a walk, or flip on HGTV to relax. I might even lie down for a few minutes and close my eyes to rest. If I'm hungry I might need to get a snack before I talk with anyone. But Jesus, though hungry and tired, focused completely and offered what the Samaritan woman needed most: full presence and complete love.

As a Samaritan woman, she had experienced racial prejudice and oppression from the Jews, who felt contempt for the Samaritans. On top of that, the men in her life hadn't treated her with honor either. Jesus, however, was different. He didn't look down on her or follow the social norms of His day. Don't you love that about Him? I sure do!

Jesus consistently looked beyond labels and stereotypes to see the hearts of those who needed His undivided attention. He drew them out, addressed their deepest needs, and focused completely on them. In doing so, Jesus offered every individual the invaluable gift of dignity and worth. His listening ears and attentive stance spoke volumes into broken lives: "You are precious and worth listening to!"

As I think about my relationships, that's the message I want to send. Isn't that the type of message you want to speak to the people in your life? Your co-workers. Your friends. Your neighbors. Your husband. Your children. All of them need to hear, "You're precious and worth listening to!"

In our fast-paced, technology-crazed, overstimulated society, how do we send that message? Do we create a bitmoji that looks like us and send a text that says, "BFF, you're precious to me"? That's definitely an option. But I have a few other suggestions as well.

Communicating, "You're precious to me!"

When our kids were little and I tucked them into bed at night, my last words as I headed out of their rooms were, "I love you. You're precious to me!" I wanted them to know beyond the shadow of a doubt how precious they were. Even though my kids are all grown, married, and have children of their own, I still want them to know they are precious. I want Steve to know that as well. One of the best ways I can show my loved ones how important they are to me is by limiting my distractions and offering them my undivided attention. I don't always do this well, but I'm moving in the right direction, and you can as well with a few intentional choices:

Eliminate Hurry

Have you noticed? We're addicted to hurry. Our internal time clock is wound tight. Our sense of hurry distracts us from listening to those around us because we're in a panic to get on with life. We rush our kids out the door to school, soccer, music lessons, and dance recitals. Our next appointment looms so we race to be the first one in line at Starbucks to beat the traffic on the way to work. When a traffic light slows us down, we don't pass up the opportunity to scan email quickly on our phones so we don't miss something important. In the midst of all our hurry, we've lost the ability to sit and listen in a relaxed and unhurried manner. In order to regain the skill of being fully attentive, we need to ruthlessly eliminate hurry.

Leighton Ford, brother-in-law of Billy Graham, once gave that advice to my husband, Steve. Steve was in a crazy season of ministry. It felt like he was pulled in a million directions with too much to do, too many people to see, and too many deadlines to meet. He met with Leighton to seek counsel on how to stay intimate with God while juggling the demands of ministry. Leighton answered that the key to Steve's spiritual depth would be his ability to "ruthlessly eliminate hurry." Those words have stuck with both Steve and me. Recently, I discovered that Dallas Willard originally come up with that advice. I'm sure glad Leighton passed it along to my hubby.

When you live in a continual state of hurry, you're caught up in thinking about the next thing on your to-do list and the next event on your Google calendar. Your mind racing full tilt, you're not able to focus on the person in front of you and fully receive what they're trying to communicate. Instead, slow down and focus.

Let Go of Multitasking

For years we've prided ourselves on our ability to multitask, but that's coming back to bite us in the relationship department. We can't listen well while checking email, sending text messages, or updating a Facebook status. We may be saying, "Uh huh, I'm listening," while scrolling through our email, but the truth is we're really not.

A few years ago my young grandson Joshy was spending the day with me. When my son, Josiah, came to pick Joshy up after work, Joshy was excited to see him. Josiah is usually a very attentive daddy, but on this particular day work had been challenging and Josiah's stress level had been rising. Sipping coffee, scanning email messages on his phone, and processing his day with me all at the same time, he didn't notice Joshy running around his feet. Joshy kept saying, "Daddy, look at me! Watch this!" Finally, in utter desperation, Joshy grabbed Josiah's phone out of his hand, put it down on the coffee table, and said, "Daddy, phone down. Watch me!" Josiah and I both cracked up and became more focused on Joshy's tricks. Sometimes it takes a verbal two-year-old to speak the truth. The bottom line is that multitasking doesn't work if you want others to feel heard and valued.

Block Your Time

Instead of trying to do two things at one time, I've learned the value of blocking my time. I set aside time for specific tasks and events rather than letting all my pressure spill over into every hour of the day. For example, after I wake up in the morning I spend time with God. I set aside thirty to forty-five minutes for exercise. I set aside several hours for writing and other hours for meeting with people. I am easily distracted, so I know I need to be disciplined. I'm learning I must set aside blocks of time to answer emails and check social media. If I don't, the tyranny of the urgent controls my life, and time with people who are important to me gets hijacked.

Those of you with toddlers at home will naturally want to connect with others on social media. It's a great way to eliminate feelings of isolation and loneliness. Enjoy social media, but set limits for yourself so that the little people in your life feel heard.

If you've recently relocated to a new community, it may feel more comfortable to fill your hours with social media because you feel lonely, rather than reaching out and getting to know your neighbors. But social media can easily eat up the hours you might invest in new friendships. Enjoy social media but set limits.

Similarly, set limits on your work. Don't let work deadlines or email rule your life. Be willing to unplug to be with those you love.

Minimize Your Stress

Recently Steve said to me, "Hey, babe, I think you've lost some hearing." Now, that's completely possible, but after further reflection I realized that I was feeling stressed over some pending deadlines. As a result, my hearing was suffering. Did you know that when you're stressed out you don't hear as well? It may be partly because you're not focusing, but research shows that stress can actually affect your ability to hear. "Reduced hearing, deafness in the ear can also be caused by persistently elevated stress."[2] Shocking, huh? If stress can limit our hearing, imagine what it can do to the rest of our bodies! I'm just sayin'.

We're more stressed out than ever. "Researchers from Carnegie Mellon University analyzed data from 1983, 2006 and 2009, and found people's self-reported stress levels have increased 10–30% in the last three decades."[3] With our stress levels on the rise, we need to develop techniques to manage the pressure, or our ability to listen to others will be lost.

We talked about recognizing the symptoms of stress in chapter 2. Beyond recognizing the symptoms, we need to consider how to handle our stress, because my guess is that the pressure in your life and mine isn't going to diminish. Here are a few strategies I use to manage my stress so that stress doesn't manage me:

- **Have face time with God.** When we think of face time, we think of the app on our phones that allows us to see the person we are talking with more clearly. When I have face time with God, my goal is to see Him more clearly. I know that in order to cope with the craziness of my schedule, I need daily times of reflection on who God is and how He feels about me. I listen to music that points me toward Him and reminds me of His steady love and faithfulness in my life. I read a portion of my Bible, which jogs my memory about the goodness of God. I usually write in a journal a reflection on whatever Scripture I read. That helps me remember through the day that God is on my side.

- **Prioritize exercise.** "Exercise in almost any form acts as a stress reliever."[4] God simply didn't design our bodies to be sedentary. When you get moving, your endorphins kick it up a notch and your body handles whatever stress you're facing. Jump on the treadmill, take a walk, go for a hike or swim. Get moving, and you'll find your stress is easier to manage.

- **Create space for beauty.** Our souls were designed with a need for beauty. When you're stressed out, it may be a signal that you're craving beauty.

    Several years ago, Steve and I were visiting friends in India. The town in which our friends lived was crowded and chaotic. One night when we were out to dinner, they told us that when the noise, dirt, and confusion feels overwhelming, they treat themselves to dinner at a luxurious hotel with beautiful gardens. They take the time to eat and then they simply walk through the quiet gardens and allow their eyes to drink in all the beauty. By the time they return to their apartment, their souls feel refreshed. How wise!

    When the demands of your life are piling up, take a breather. Go somewhere that holds beauty: a park, a beach, an art museum, or a flower garden. Let your spirit, soul, and body refresh as you delight in the beauty all around.

- **Remember how to play.** Play is important for childhood development, but it's also critical to our well-being as adults. Who knew? It turns out that playing can elevate your mood, increase your ability to bond with others, help you be more productive at work, and heighten your creativity. So the next time you're stressed out and uptight, grab some bubbles or sidewalk chalk, go for a bike ride, or pull out a board game! You'll be doing yourself and your loved ones a favor because after you release some of your stress, you'll be able to be more present to those you love.

Recently, a couple of our grandkids were over and they had made a roadway out of duct tape on our carpeted floor. After playing for quite a while with their cars, their parents told the boys they had to pull up the tape because they had to leave soon. Steve joined in the fun of pulling the tape off the carpet and showed the boys how to make duct tape balls. Before I knew it, the duct tape was flying all over the family room as Ty and Joshy were trying to attack Papa with duct tape balls. Papa hid behind chairs and pummeled the boys back. Laughter filled the room as a duct tape war broke out. Papa finally surrendered, everyone went home calm and happy, and Papa smiled for a long time after. My conclusion is that a few moments of pure silliness goes a long way in relieving stress.

- **Know when you need a break.** I'm the type of person who sets very high standards for herself. A recovering "people pleaser," I found it difficult at first to realize I couldn't be a great listener to everyone. I enjoy people and I love making new friends. But according to research done by Robin Dunbar, an anthropologist and psychiatrist, a person can only handle 150 to 200 casual friends. Within that 150 or so, there is a circle of about fifty whom you might call "good friends." Narrowing that down, there is a group of about fifteen whom you might confide in, and a circle of five who are your most intimate support group.[5] Some probably feel those numbers are too high. Others might feel they're too low. Either way, the important thing is to understand that you can't be close friends with everyone. Friendships also experience seasons. There are seasons when your friendship with someone might be very intense, and other seasons when the friendship might be more casual. Friendships ebb and flow.

What happens when we try to cultivate deep relationships with everyone? Our brains literally become exhausted and our listening ability diminishes. If you're feeling overwhelmed, disconnected, spacey, and unable to focus, pull back. Consider the people in your social circles. Which of them would you consider to be casual friends? Which do you consider deep friends, and which do you consider kindred spirit, "pour your heart out to" intimate friends? Think through which of your friends energize you and which relationships drain you. It might be time to pull back a bit. I'll warn you—this is tough. Some will be disappointed.

It's good to remember in this process that boundaries were God's idea (Psalm 104:9). What do I mean by boundaries? Boundaries are simply limits you set for yourself. They help define what's your responsibility and what's not. When you set boundaries, you establish what you need for your own physical, emotional, and spiritual well-being.

You can't be everyone's BFF. I know; I've tried. Does that mean you should never take time to listen to a stranger or an acquaintance? No. We'll talk about that in the next chapter. But for now, understand your limits and know that most of your energy for attentive listening should be spent on the relationships that you value the most.

Our brains are complicated and limited. They can only handle so much stress and stimulation. If you want to be an attentive listener to others, you'll have to figure out ways to minimize your stress. Otherwise, you'll be too burned out to listen effectively to anyone.

Savor the Moment

Every now and then I pull out photo albums from when my kids were little, and I realize again how quickly time flies. It seems as though just yesterday they were learning to ride bikes, digging in the sand, playing soccer, and competing in swim meets. Now they're all raising their kids. I'm more aware than ever of how fast time flies, so I've started a silent practice of taking screenshots in my mind. What do I mean? I pause and take a moment to simply capture the moment. Let me give you an example. As I write this, I've just come home from my four-year-old granddaughter Selah's birthday party. During the party, I stood holding my little granddaughter Rayna and watching the chaos of little children run through the backyard. I paused and took in the scene with all five senses. I snuggled Rayna close, feeling her little cheek against mine. I watched all the little kiddos racing through the yard. I listened to the sounds of children laughing and adults talking. I smelled the fresh scent of lavender on baby Rayna. I whispered a prayer, "Lord, help me not to forget this moment." I try to do the same thing when we have Sunday dinner as a family. The grandkids may be running through the house, the adults talking, one or more of the babies or toddlers might be crying, but the chaos is wonderful. It's the sound of family, love, and life, and I don't want to miss a minute. I want to be fully present and savor the memories, cherishing them in my heart.

Life Is Short

Life is short. Kids grow up and people grow old. Take time to live life fully present and attentive to those you love. What you invest now will determine the payoff later. If you're raising toddlers, how you listen to them now will often determine how much they talk to you as teens. How you listen to your teens will determine what type of relationship you have with them as adults. It's never too late, but it might take a lot of work to change when they're older.

If you have aging parents, create the space to listen to them, because you don't know how much longer you'll have them. Draw them out and take the time to listen. One of the sweetest times I had with my precious in-laws was when I asked my dear father-in-law what it was like to attend boarding school in Canada while his parents were on the mission field in Africa.

Dad answered by opening letters he had written to his parents and read them to me. The letters spoke of how much he loved hockey and how he had gotten into trouble at school for throwing a football through the window. After we read the letters, Dad pulled out photo albums and told me about falling in love with Mom and their time dating. He told me about the Scriptures he loved and verses he memorized. I will always treasure that conversation in my heart.

Moments pass quickly. Our lives are a mere vapor that appears for a little while and then vanishes (James 4:14). We are never able to go back and retrieve lost moments, so be attentive. Eliminate the distractions that are robbing your ability to listen. Offer your full presence to those you love.

I discovered this prayer written by Rachel Wojo on the Internet. Before we dive into the last chapter of this book and talk about being available . . . pause. Pray the words of this prayer and savor a moment with God.

Dear Father,
Thank you for this exact point in time.
Sometimes I struggle
To enjoy the gift of the present.
I push forward before your timing is perfect
And then feel the pain of rushing.
My spirit longs to savor the moment
While my mind scrambles to snatch the next minute.
Will you slow my heart to beat your rhythm?
Will you sync my step to mirror your tempo?
May my spirit fail to chase
After the next beautiful experience
Until I've unwrapped the gift of right now—
The present.
Amen.[6]

Listening to God

1. Read Psalm 84:1. The psalmist talks about God's presence. How do you best experience God's presence in your life?

2. What does it look like for you to be fully present to God when you can't see Him or touch Him?

3. Psalm 116:2 in the New Living Translation reads, "Because he bends down to listen, I will pray as long as I have breath!" What does this verse tell you about how God is attentive to you while you're praying? Close your eyes and imagine God bending down to listen to you. What does it feel like for you to have God's complete, undivided attention?

Listening to Your Heart

4. What drives you to check email or social media constantly?

5. What distracts you most often from listening attentively to others?

6. Do you struggle with an internal sense of hurry? If so, where do you think that comes from?

7. Take some focused time to analyze your friend circles:
    • Who is in your 150 to 200 group of casual friends?
    • Who are your fifty good friends?
    • Who are the people in your group of fifteen close friends?
    • Who are the five people you would pour your heart out to?

Listening to Others

Choose one of these activities:

8. Take an eight-hour period of any given day and try completely unplugging. (No computer, phone, TV, or any other technology.) Instead, focus on listening. Journal your feelings about this experience.

9. Set a date night with your spouse this week, or if you're single, set aside time to be with a good friend. Turn off your phone, the TV, and any other form of noise. Do something that doesn't involve technology. Make it your goal for the evening to be a great, attentive listener. Sometime after, record your feelings in your journal. What new fact did you learn about your spouse or friend?

10

Be Available

If God only used perfect people, nothing would get
done. God will use anybody if you're available.

—Rick Warren

At the beginning of this book, I vulnerably shared with you
a conversation I had with my teen daughter, who found the
courage to speak truth into my life about my listening skills. Looking back, I'm so thankful Bethany was honest with me. That conversation shaped the trajectory of our relationship as she moved
into adulthood. As I began to listen more intentionally, Bethany
began to open her heart more. She felt more connected. My actions showed her that I loved her and wanted to hear her heart, and
as a result, she felt safe enough to talk. Now Bethany and I have
meaningful conversations every day. I love hearing what's going
on in her life and family. In fact, Bethany helped to edit this book
and has shaped much of the content. Why? Because I value her
thoughts and ideas. Now, mind you, I haven't become a perfect
listener. I'm still working on my skills, but the effort I've put in
has paid off in my other relationships as well.

As God shaped my heart to listen more effectively to those I love, He also expanded my horizons. I began to wonder, *What would it look like for God to use me as a "listening conduit" for those who need His love?* A conduit is a pipe or tube that allows water or other things to pass through. I wanted the love of Christ to flow unhindered through my listening ears.

In order for God to use me as a conduit of His love, I needed to be ready and available.

Ready and Available

After reading this book, you're ready to be a great listener. You have the skills and the know-how you need. Hopefully, you've practiced those skills and you've seen improvement. Not perfection, but improvement. The question now is, Are you available?

The word *available* means to be "ready for use, accessible."[1] Beyond know-how, it involves willingness. Think about it. Understanding the practices that make you a better listener is great, but if you're not accessible, what difference do those practices make in deepening your relationships?

- If you're not available to your spouse or kids, what good is the 15-minute rule?
- If you're not available to ask questions, why bother learning how?
- If you're not available when a friend walks through seasons of grief, why develop strong empathy skills?
- If you're not available to listen during conflict, how will the conflict be transformational?

I believe God wants us to be available to deepen our relationships and to carry the presence of Christ. The truth is that you and I were created on purpose and for a purpose. We weren't created to simply drift through life and make ourselves happy. According to the Bible, you were created by God to do specific works that God has designed for you to do (Ephesians 2:10). Jesus came to earth so that we would better understand the love of God. Now we are to carry His love to the world around us by exemplifying the love of Christ. One of the most profound ways we demonstrate the love of Christ is by our availability to listen.

As I've thought about what this might look like in my life and yours, I've narrowed it down to five simple principles. We could call them the Five Be's of Availability.

The Five Be's of Availability

Be Reliable

One of the most beautiful qualities in a spouse, friend, family member, or co-worker is reliability. Relational wisdom from Proverbs warns that "one who has unreliable friends soon comes to ruin" (Proverbs 18:24). In order to be surrounded by reliable friends, I need to be a reliable friend.

Each of us needs a supportive community surrounding us that we know we can count on when life feels turbulent. These are the close friends or family members you can call in the middle of the night when life falls apart. These are the friends who have proven themselves faithful over time. You can count on these friends to listen when you feel confused, angry, hurt, or simply jumbled. They listen and allow you to process. They don't judge, break your confidence, or give up on you when you're not at your best. If you have a friend like that, cherish that relationship, because it's a great treasure!

I have several close friends who are as reliable as the day is long. I know I can count on them to help me at a moment's notice. They have walked with me, prayed with me, comforted me, and listened to me. Some of these friends have been in my life for years; they knew me when my kids were small and supported me when my kids were teens. Others have been there with me through the challenges of ministry life, cancer, and other trials. They continue to remain a steady support, and they are precious to me because they have been reliable.

I want to be reliable as well—for Steve, my kids and grandkids, my friends, and my ministry partners. I know I can't be that for everyone because there's not enough of me to go around. As we talked about in the last chapter, I need to set boundaries. I can be reliable for some, but not all. I want each of my close friends to know they can count on me to listen, encourage, comfort, and support. Through different seasons my circumstances may change, but I want the overall tenor of my life to speak reliability to my family and friends. I asked my Facebook friends what came to mind for them when they heard the word *reliable*. Here are a few truths of reliability that were repeated often:

- Reliable friends keep confidences; you know your story is safe with them.
- Reliable friends lay aside their agenda to hear yours.
- Reliable friends cheer for you when you succeed and pick you up when you fail.
- Reliable friends rejoice with you when life is going well and weep with you when life stinks.

Tracy commented that when she thought about reliability, her dad came to mind. Here's what Tracy told me about her dad.

Reliable. My dad comes to my mind. He's predictably reliable. When I was recently diagnosed with breast cancer, I called my dad, who lives one and a half hours' drive from me, and we had a few tears and chatted on the phone for a bit. We said we loved each other and hung up. A few hours later, my seventy-four-year-old dad was at my doorstep because he had to see his baby. I'm fifty. Ha ha. But I know I can count on my dad. He's there. He's reliable. He is consistent and predictably reliable and I'm sooooooo grateful to

156

have him and others like him in my life. Now I gotta call my dad and tell him I love him.

Tracy's dad is reliable. He has put in the work to consistently listen to his daughter over time. That's why she reached out and called him when she was diagnosed with breast cancer. The depth of their relationship allowed him the freedom to surprise her and show up at her door. She appreciated and felt comforted by that surprise because her dad had consistently listened in a selfless, available way.

Credibility builds over time. As you faithfully show your husband, your kids, your friends, your siblings, or your co-workers that you are ready to listen, you'll prove that you're reliable. And do you know what? Reliability pays great dividends. Do you know that the happiest people in old age are those who have cultivated deep relationships over the years? These are the elderly people walking around with big smiles on their faces. Their relationships are strong, and people enjoy being with them because over the years they proved they were reliable listeners.

Be Intentional

You were intentional about picking up this book and learning new listening skills. Congratulations! Your intentionality will speak volumes to the people you love. The challenge is to stay intentional as you move forward—not just in your close relationships, but also to those who need to know God loves them. Make the intentional choice and look for opportunities.

One of the intentional habits that Steve and I practice is cultivating connections with servers at the restaurants we visit most often. We also do this with baristas at the Starbucks where we're regulars. We do this for two reasons. First, it allows us the opportunity to share Christ's love, and second, it makes us better neighbors. Jesus wants us to seek peace and pursue it in our neighborhoods and communities. As we talked about in the last chapter, you can't be

BFFs with everyone, but you can take a moment or two to listen to the people in your community.

Ivan is one of our favorite servers at a Mexican restaurant where we often eat. A few years ago we asked him how we could pray for him. At the time, he was getting ready to have surgery, so we prayed with him and for him. A few weeks later when we went back, we remembered to ask how his surgery went and how he was feeling. Again, we asked how we could pray for him, and this time he shared with us the story of his friend who was battling cancer. Steve and I prayed for his friend. Months later we went back and asked Ivan about his friend. Ivan told us his friend had passed away. Her death had been difficult on Ivan's entire family. He showed us the video that was shown at her funeral. Again, Steve and I prayed for Ivan and his wife. Whenever we walk into that restaurant, Ivan seeks us out and gives us a huge hug. We continue to pray that Ivan will grow deeper in knowing the love of Christ.

Be Prepared

I have found it helpful to prepare myself to listen when I'm on my way to meet a friend or going to an event. What do I mean? There are times when I have a lot going on in my world—deadlines, pressures, stressors, or concerns. As I drive to a coffee date or meeting, I do an internal check, considering what's on my mind. I'm well aware of my triggers. For example, if someone starts to share with me a story about an adoption, I'm likely to dive in and tell them all about my adopted grandson. Or if someone starts telling me about a deadline they're facing at work, I might feel tempted to dive in and tell them about my deadline. That's why I need to contain. I mentally picture putting all my "stuff" in a box so that I have created the space in my mind to listen to the other person and completely focus on them.

I'm guessing it's the same for you. Your worries might be different from mine, and you might have different deadlines, but you've got stuff. The next time you're meeting friends for dinner or meeting a co-worker for lunch, imagine putting your worries, concerns, stressors, and triggers in a box. Listen to your friends first. I'm not suggesting that you don't share your concerns, or that you should never share your concerns first. That's all part of relationship. But when you're working on your listening skills, practice putting your own concerns in a box. You can re-open your box of worries after you've left the event.

Be Flexible

If you're going to be available to be a listening conduit, you'll need to be flexible. At times opportunities will arise when it's not convenient to listen.

Steve is a strategic thinker. He's a visionary who knows where he's going. When he's leading an organization he can tell you where he's headed for the next five, ten, and even twenty years. But in our marriage relationship, he values spontaneity. That was a stretch for me in our first few years together. I would have a plan in place for the evening and Steve would call me from work with a completely different plan in mind. Honestly, I wasn't very flexible.

At times, I'd be preparing to teach a Bible study or to speak at a women's event, and my man would come home with a lot on his mind and want to go somewhere quiet to talk. At first it was very hard for me to lay aside whatever I was working on. I would almost panic worrying about not finishing my project on time. Gradually, the Lord showed me that if I would prioritize listening to Steve, He would provide the wisdom and prep time to finish creative projects.

The same principle holds true in the realm of being a good neighbor. For many years, Steve and I were so caught up in ministry life that our neighbors hardly ever saw us other than our car pulling in and out of the driveway. Sometimes our neighbors need to talk, and we need to slow down long enough to listen.

Remember the neighbor I told you about in the beginning of this book who I mistakenly thought didn't like me? Well, the other day I was driving off, and I admit I was in a bit of a hurry. (I know, I need to ruthlessly eliminate hurry . . .) When my neighbor Clarice flagged me down, it was not a convenient time. I stopped and rolled down my window and Clarice began to talk. Her words astounded me. Clarice had seen the Realtor sign in the front of our house, and she asked me if we were moving. When I told her yes, we were moving, she began to get emotional. She said, "Oh Becky, I'm going to miss you. I feel safer here with you next door." She began to tell me again how far away her kids live and that her mother is dying. After we ended our conversation, I drove away deep in thought and prayed, *Lord, I really haven't been the greatest neighbor to Clarice. But thank you that you used me to help her feel safe. Please continue to help me to be flexible and slow down long enough to listen to those who need your love.*

Be Alert to Divine Appointments

Divine appointments are those conversations that are divinely scheduled and orchestrated by God for His purposes. Often they begin with a nudge from the Holy Spirit. As I've said, the nudge might come at an inconvenient time. It's easy to rationalize that you're too busy, tired, stressed, or whatever to respond. But if you're alert, with your ears listening for opportunities, God will use you in extraordinary ways.

Several years ago, our daughter Keri was flying home from college after taking her final exams. Exhausted, she found her seat on the plane and pulled out a magazine. The beautiful woman next to her opened a conversation about the magazine, and it became apparent to Keri that she really wanted to talk. Keri felt the Holy Spirit nudge her, so she put her magazine away. She asked the beautiful woman next to her, "What do you do for a living?" The young woman responded that she was an actress. Keri had taken some acting classes in high school and saw the opportunity for connection. She told the woman that she herself used to act. As they continued in their conversation, the woman confessed that she was a porn star.

Keri whispered a prayer for wisdom, and then sensitively asked a few more questions. "How did you get into that line of business? How does it make you feel?"

In response to Keri's sensitivity, Jessica began to share her story. She had been part of an abstinence campaign as a teen. On the last night of the campaign, she was raped. Feeling confused and desperate and disappointed with God for not protecting her, she decided to enter the industry. Through many tears she shared her story. Keri listened with tears in her own eyes and asked if she could pray with Jessica. As the plane landed, Keri held Jessica's hand and prayed that God would reassure Jessica of His love, and the two young women vowed to stay in touch.

For several years, Keri and the rest of our family prayed faithfully for Jessica. Amazingly, we recently found out that Jessica is now out of the industry and speaking out against trafficking! Jessica said that during her time in the industry, God strategically placed many Christians on planes next to her, and each one who listened to her story prayed for her. Each one was a divine appointment ordained by God to bring Jessica back to himself.

As I think about Jessica, I wonder what would have happened if the people God placed next to her on planes had not responded or listened? Or what if they had decided to preach to Jessica and attempted to fix all her problems? The outcome could have been very different.

Divine appointments are orchestrated by God, and they're not out of the ordinary. But they're easily missed if you're walking through life in a fog and unavailable. I get it. Life can feel over-whelming, and it's easy to feel so swamped by our own problems and challenges that we're not aware of what's happening in the lives of others. Or we can feel as though the problems of others are too big, too tragic, or too devastating for us to listen. Every day we hear stories of violence and horror on the evening news.

It's easy to get anesthetized to the pain and problems people face. The temptation is for us to shut down emotionally and check out mentally. But what if God wants us to wake up and make a difference with our listening ears?

Have you ever been on anesthesia? I sure have. Over a period of five years, I had seven surgeries. I remember walking through life feeling as though I wasn't quite there. During that season, my kids would joke with me, "Mom, the lights are on but nobody's home," referring to my brain. No kidding! When you're recovering from surgery, fogginess is the norm, but that's not the way I want to live my life as a regular pattern. I want to live life alert and available to God. I want to be ready to step into any divine appointment He orchestrates. But that means I have to wake up and live my life alert to God and His desire for the people around me.

A Closing Challenge

As we close out this book, I wish we could sit and have a cup of coffee together. I'd love to hear your heart and how you've processed all the thoughts in this book. I'd love to hear how you've shown empathy to others, how you've drawn out their stories and valued their thoughts and opinions. We probably can't do that, but I would love to hear from you. So please, stay in touch and share your thoughts on my blog, www.beckyharling.com. Let me know how you're doing in the realm of listening. I believe with all my heart that God wants us all to continue growing in our listening skills so that He can use us as the listening conduits He desires us to be. He longs to have us be available to Him so that His love can flow through us to our friends, co-workers, husbands, children, grandkids, neighbors, parents, siblings, and even strangers.

I know your relationships are important to you, otherwise you wouldn't have finished this book. You cherish and value the people you love just like I do. As you lay this book down, I challenge you to continue growing in the listening realm. Don't get too uptight about doing it perfectly. Just focus on taking tiny intentional steps to be a more attentive listener. As you're taking those tiny steps, know that I'm taking them with you and cheering for you! The effort you put in will pay off. As you listen, people will talk. Your relationships will thrive and flourish, and God will use you to help others feel His love.

Listening to God

1. Read 2 Timothy 4:2. If our actions speak louder than our words, what does it look like to "preach God's love" with our ears?

2. Read 1 Thessalonians 5:11. What does this verse speak to you about being available to others?

3. As you reflect back on your journey through this book, what is one truth that God has spoken to you?

Listening to Your Heart

4. After reading this book, what are two tangible tips you will begin using as you listen to others? How will you implement them moving forward?

5. Describe what it would be like for you to be used by God as a listening conduit.

6. Write a letter to yourself that you can open in five years, describing the type of listener you would like to be. Keep the letter in a safe place, and in five years you can measure your growth.

Listening to Others

7. Make it your goal to ask either a server at a restaurant or a barista at a coffee shop how you can pray for them. Record your experience in the space below.

8. Who do you need to be more available to? What would need to change in your life for you to be more accessible to that person?

Notes

Chapter 1: I Dare You to Ask!

1. Maya Angelou, Twitter post, May 18, 2013, 7:32 pm, https://twitter.com /DrMayaAngelou?ref_src=twsrc%5Etfw.

2. Dietrich Bonhoeffer, *Life Together* (New York: Harper &Row, 1954), 98–99.

Chapter 2: Raise Your Self-Awareness

1. John Savage, *Listening & Caring Skills* (Nashville: Abington Press, 1996), 46–47.

2. Rip Tilden, Makarios Consulting, June 25, 2012, http://makariosconsult ing.com/listening-with-humility-the-most-powerful-leadership-tool-is-at-the -top-of-the-leadership-skills-list/.

Chapter 3: Honor Another's Story

1. Kirsti A. Dyer, MD, MS, FAAETS, "The Importance of Telling (and Listen-ing) to the Story," Journey of Hearts, http://journeyofhearts.org/kirstimd/tell story.htm.

2. William Barclay, *The New Daily Study Bible Series: Gospel of Matthew*, rev ed (Louisville, KY: Westminster John Knox Press, 2001).

Chapter 4: Silence Your Inner Fixer

1. Strengths Test, http://www.strengthstest.com/strengthsfinderthemes /strengths-themes.html.

2. Dale Carnegie, *How to Win Friends and Influence People* (New York: Simon and Schuster, 1981).

3. Win Couchman, "Cross-Generational Relationships," Speaking at Women for Christ, 1983, Winter Break (tape available from Domain Communications, Wheaton, IL).

4. www.youtube.com/watch?v=otH3KZwVS7w

Chapter 5: Ask Great Questions

1. John Maxwell, *Everyone Communicates Few Connect* (Nashville: Thomas Nelson, 2010), 133.

2. Belle Beth Cooper, "5 Habits of Highly Effective Communicators," Buffer, August 8, 2013, https://blog.bufferapp.com/why-talking-about-ourselves-is-as-rewarding-as-sex-the-science-of-conversations.

3. www.youtube.com/watch?v=ogGOlGswStA

Chapter 6: Offer Empathy, Validate Feelings

1. *Psychology Today*, https://www.psychologytoday.com/basics/empathy.

2. Strong's Concordance #4834.

3. Carin Rubenstein and Margaret Jaworski, "When Husbands Rate Second," *Family Circle*, May 5, 1987, 105.

4. Dee Brestin, *The Friendships of Women* (Colorado Springs: Cook, 2008), 109.

5. Dee Brestin, 108.

6. Strong's Concordance #5162.

Chapter 7: Watch Your Nonverbals—They're Speaking Loudly

1. Kevin Hogan, "Read and Interpret Body Language Like the Body Language Expert," www.kevinhogan.com/bodylanguage.htm

2. "Non-Verbal Communication," Skills You Need, www.skillsyouneed.com/ips/nonverbal-communication.html

3. Jeanne Segal, PhD, Melinda Smith, MA, Greg Boose, and Jaelline Jaffe, PhD, "Nonverbal Communication," HelpGuide, www.helpguide.org/articles/relationships/nonverbal-communication.htm.

4. *While You Were Sleeping*, directed by Jon Turteltaub, Hollywood Pictures, 1995.

5. Michael Hyatt, "5 Reasons You Should Smile More as a Leader," http://michaelhyatt.com/5-reasons-you-should-smile-more-as-a-leader.html.

6. James G Friesen, PhD, E. James Wilder, PhD, Anne M. Bierling, MA, Rick Koepcke, MA, Maribeth Poole, MA, *Living From the Heart Jesus Gave You* (Pasadena, CA: Shepherd's House, 2004), 22–23.

7. Kris Cole, "Stuck in a rut? Six tips to pull you out," Cole Management Theory and Practice, October 9, 2015, https://colemanagement.wordpress.com /2015/10/09/stuck-in-a-rut-six-tips-to-pull-you-out.

8. John Maxwell, *Everyone Communicates, Few Connect* (Nashville: Thomas Nelson, 2010), 55, 58.

9. "What Is Your Body Language Saying?" *Real Simple*, http://www.realsimple .com/health/mind-mood/reading-body-language/how-read-faces.

10. www.youtube.com/watch?v=vpWTCHN_cy4

11. www.youtube.com/watch?v=aG04JhgpI7g

Chapter 8: Seek to Understand During Conflict

1. Elmer Towns, "How Did the Apostle Peter Die?" *Bible Sprout*, http://www .biblesprout.com/articles/bible/apostle-peter-die/.

2. Lawrence W. Wilson, "6 Ways to Transform Conflict," http://michaelhyatt .com/6-ways-to-transform-conflict.html.

3. Poppy Smith, *Why Can't He Be More Like Me?* (Eugene, OR: Harvest House Publishers, 2012), 118.

4. Mark Goulston, *Just Listen* (New York: AMACOM, 2010), 64.

5. Ibid., 65.

6. Prayer of Saint Francis, see "Make Me an Instrument of Your Peace," www .catholic.org/prayers/prayer.php?p=134.

Chapter 9: Let Go of Distractions

1. Henri Nouwen, *Out of Solitude* (Notre Dame, IN: Ave Maria Press, 2004), 39.

2. Jim Folk and Marilyn Folk, BScN, Anxiety Symptoms, January 10, 2017, www.anxietycentre.com/anxiety-symptoms/reduced-hearing-deafness.shtml.

3. Meghan Neal, "Stress levels soar in America by up to 30% in 30 years," *New York Daily News*, Saturday, June 16, 2012, www.nydailynews.com/news /national/stress-levels-soar-america-30–30-years-article-1.1096918.

4. Mayo Clinic, "Stress Management," Healthy Lifestyle, http://www.mayo clinic.org/healthy-lifestyle/stress-management/in-depth/exercise-and-stress/art -20044469.

5. Maria Konnikova, "The Limits of Friendship," *The New Yorker*, October 7, 2014, http://www.newyorker.com/science/maria-konnikova/social-media-aff ect-math-dunbar-number-friendships.

6. Rachel Wojo, "A Prayer to Savor the Moment," Encouraging Fresh Faith, http://rachelwojo.com/a-prayer-to-savor-the-moment.

Chapter 10: Be Available

1. Available, http://www.dictionary.com/browse/available?s=t.

Acknowledgments

My Special Thanks to . . .

My husband, Steve. Babe, you are such an incredible leader and life partner! You believe in me, encourage me, challenge me, and cheer for me as I seek to live out my calling. I love the adventure we are living together. Thanks for giving me the world. No one I know has a greater global heart than you! I love you!

My Kids:

Bethany, this book would have never happened had it not been for you! Thanks for challenging me to become a more attentive listener and for allowing me to process the concepts taught in this book with you. I love your heart for adoption. Truly it mirrors the heart of God. I love you and am so proud of you!

Josiah, I love watching God pour gifts of leadership and wisdom through your life. You have extraordinary ability to influence organizations to think more missionally for the glory of God. Seeing your ability to plan conferences and speak with Dad brings tears to my eyes! I love you and am so proud of you!

Stefanie, what a joy to hear you speak and teach the Word of God! You are an incredible Bible teacher! I love watching your heart for your family and also for women. You are one of the most passionate women I know. I love you and am so proud of you!

Kerith, what an anointing is on your life. You have such an extraordinary ability to lead people into the presence of God. It's been so fun to see you step so confidently into motherhood and also into leading other moms towards a deeper walk with Christ. I love you and am so proud of you!

My Kids-in-Love:

Chris, I love your gentle servant heart both for Bethany and your precious boys. You are such an attentive husband and father. I love the way you and Bethany lead the adoption ministry together. Thanks for modeling Christ so well! I love you and am proud of you!

Shaina, I love your gentleness and your faithfulness to Christ. Your loyalty to both your family and your friends is beautiful. You're such a sweet and calm mama to your boys. Thanks for letting me process my thoughts about this book and for your continued encouragement. I love you and am proud of you!

Dave, I love your heart for Christ, your passion for the broken, and your desire for the Word. You're a great husband and dad. Thanks for encouraging Stef to use her gifts of speaking and writing. I love you and am proud of you!

Zach, I love your heart for Christ and your passion for leadership. I love hearing about what you're reading, and I love watching how God is using you. You are so intentional in your walk. Thanks for encouraging Keri to use her gifts and for being such a great dad to your kids. I love you and am proud of you!

My Grandkids:

Charlie, I love your strong heart for Jesus and how you are already praying for your friends to find Him. I love you and am proud of you.

Tyler, I love your passion for Jesus and for worshiping Him. Recently, you told me you just want to live and love like Jesus! I love you and am proud of you.

Joshua, I love how you recently told Jesus you want to follow Him for the rest of your life! You're such a strong leader already. I love you and am proud of you.

Selah, I love your heart for Jesus and how compassionate you are toward others. You sparkle and shine for Jesus in extraordinary ways! I love you and am so proud of you.

Zachary, I love how you're learning about Jesus, and I wish I had your energy! You are a world changer already! I love you and am so proud of you.

Theo, I love your fun-loving heart and your go-getter spirit. God has big plans for you and I love you so much!

Noah, I love how much you love people already, and I know God has big plans for you! I love you so much.

Rayna, I love how you are filled with so much joy and you simply smile all the time. God has big plans for you. I love you so much.

Cayden, I love how affectionate you are, and I love the way you already want to keep up with your brothers. I know God has big plans for you; I love you so much.

All the many men and women who made this book possible:

Blythe Daniels, thanks for believing in this project and for being such a great agent. Thanks for listening as I processed my idea and for steering me toward Bethany House Publishers. I love your heart!

Kim Bangs, thanks for seeing the potential in this book and standing with me through the finished project. What a joy to get to know you through this project!

All the men and women at Bethany House Publishers, thanks for your heart and for your confidence in this project. What a privilege to be published by you!

The John Maxwell Team, I love learning from all of you and how you continually challenge me to reach my fullest God-given potential.

The women who field-tested this book: Bethany Lindgren, Shaina Harling, Stefanie Holder, Kerith Denison, Becky Hartwell, Beth Dare, Jade Hayes, Nanci McCalister, Sharon Hanchett, Debbie Stocker, Deb Hall, Jill Geldmacher, Jill Lillard, Erika Morris, Gail Lillis, Karen Sherill, Leslie Brandow, Lauri Dennis, Sara Littlejohn, Diane Waller, Julie Jaeke, Brenda Pucket, and Bobbie Schaeperkoetter. Your feedback was invaluable, and your prayers as I wrote were amazing! Thank you from the bottom of my heart. I love each of you!

The incredible men and women who serve alongside us at Reach Beyond. What a joy and humble privilege to serve with you as we seek to be the voice and the hands of Jesus together!

About the Author

Hey, friend!

I feel like it's appropriate to call you my friend since we've journeyed through this book together. When I read a book, I like to know more about the author, so I'm assuming that's true for you as well. Here are a few facts about me: I've been married to Steve for thirty-six years. We got married two weeks after college graduation, and right after our honeymoon moved straight into a tiny church parsonage. We've spent thirty-six years in pastoral ministry, but as I've been writing this book, we've gone through a huge life transition. Steve is now the president/CEO of Reach Beyond, a nonprofit committed to being the voice and hands of Jesus around the world. Steve and I travel all over the world together. We speak both as individuals and together on topics including spiritual growth, leadership, communication, and world missions. We have four adult kids and nine grandkids, and a tenth on the way. I love having the whole family for Sunday dinners and holidays. It's wild, fun, and chaotic! I'm a certified John Maxwell speaker, coach, and trainer, and I coach those looking to improve their communication skills and those looking to improve their connection with God. I love a cup of strong coffee and a good book!

Throughout this book, I've been vulnerable about my weaknesses. I'm committed to personal growth both in my life and yours. I hope and pray that I've given you permission to be honest about your weaknesses. Only when you're honest can growth happen.

As a writer, I'm passionate about creating resources that lead to life transformation so that each reader can become the person that God created him or her to be. I invite you to check out some of the other books I've written, including *Rewriting Your Emotional Script*, *Freedom From Performing*, *The 30-Day Praise Challenge*, and *The 30-Day Praise Challenge For Parents*. I enjoy creating new resources and tools to help you in your journey toward growth. Tools such as *Listening to God*, *Listening to Your Adult Kids*, *Magnify Your Message: Unleash the Power of Personal Stories*, and others can be found at my website, www.beckyharling.com.

I've loved sharing this book with you, so I hope we'll stay connected! You can follow me on:

Facebook at www.facebook.com/beckyharlingministries
Twitter at @BeckyHarling
LinkedIn at www.linkedin.com/in/becky-harling-31605212
Instagram at BeckyHarling

By staying connected, you'll find out where and when I'll be speaking. I'd love to have you join me at an event!

Blessings and Joy,
Becky